GROWTH WITH EQUITY
THE NEW TECHNOLOGY AND
AGRARIAN CHANGE IN BENGAL

GROWTH WITH EQUITY

The New Technology and Agrarian Change in Bengal

ABHIJIT DASGUPTA

MANOHAR
1998

First published 1998

© IDPAD, 1998

ISBN 81-7304-245-4

Published by
Ajay Kumar Jain for
Manohar Publishers & Distributors
2/6 Ansari Road, Daryaganj
New Delhi 110 002

Laser typeset by
Pradeep Kumar Goel for
Aditya Prakashan, F 14/65, Model Town II
Delhi 110 009

printed at
Replika Press Pvt. Ltd.
Plot No. A-229
DSIDC Narela Indl Park
Delhi 110 040

To Professor T. Scarlett Epstein

Contents

Tables

Maps and Chart

MAPS

Acknowledgements

This is a revised version of a project report prepared for the Indian Council of Social Science Research (ICSSR) and the Netherlands Foundation for the Advancement of Tropical Research (WOTRO). I was offered a grant under their Indo-Dutch Programme on Alternatives in Development (IDPAD). The grant enabled me to do fieldwork in West Bengal and Bangladesh. I am grateful to the ICSSR and the WOTRO.

While writing this report, I have had innumerable discussions on various issues with a large number of colleagues in Delhi, West Bengal and Bangladesh. In West Bengal, Nripen Bandopadhyay, Biplab Dasgupta and Sunil Sen were most generous with their time. A large number of state government officials in Nadia, Krishnanagar and Ranaghat helped me in locating many published and unpublished official materials. The residents of village Bira spared their valuable time and helped me in every possible way. Nabarun Majumder assisted me during my fieldwork in the village and in classifying and tabulating data. I owe a great deal to all these friends.

In Bangladesh, the members of the staff at the Department of Sociology, Dhaka University shared their ideas with me. In particular, I would like to thank Anwarullah Chowdhury, Mahbub Ahmed, Tasinah Ahmed, Mansur Musa and B.K. Jahangir of the University of Dhaka. M. Alam, Bangladesh Institute of Development Studies, Ajoy Roy former Secretary of the CPB, Sanat Kumar Saha, Rajshahi University and Anwarul Karim, Lalan Academy, Kushtia helped me in many ways. Nurul Huda assisted me during my fieldwork in Naopara village and helped me at the time of data processing. I acknowledge my immense debt to all these friends in Bangladesh.

I benefitted from my discussion with a number of colleagues at the Department of Sociology, University of Delhi. I would like to thank Andre Beteille, Anand Chakravarti and Virginius Xaxa for offering me suggestions. Thanks also to Willem van Schendel, University of

Amsterdam, The Netherlands, for discussing several theoretical issues at length. Finally, I should like to add that IDPAD does not take responsibility for the facts stated, opinions expressed and conclusions reached in this publication.

ABHIJIT DASGUPTA

Abbreviations

BAES	:	Bureau of Applied Economics and Statistics
BADC	:	Bangladesh Agricultural Development Corporation
BDO	:	Block Development Officer
BRAC	:	Bangladesh Rural Advancement Council
BARD	:	Bangladesh Academy for Rural Development
BPKS	:	Bengal Provincial Kisan Sabha
BRRI	:	Bangladesh Rice Research Institute
BWDB	:	Bangladesh Water Development Board
CADC	:	Comprehensive Area Development Corporation
CPB	:	Communist Party of Bangladesh
CPI (M)	:	Communist Party of India (Marxist)
CS	:	Cadestral Survey
DA	:	Department of Agriculture
DRDA	:	District Rural Development Agency
DTW	:	Deep Tubewell
EAA	:	Estate Acquisition Act
EBSATA	:	East Bengal State Acquisition and Tenancy Act
FMSR	:	Farm Management Survey Report
GKP	:	Ganges-Kobadak Project
GSK	:	Gono Sastho Kendra
HYV	:	High Yield Varities
IRDP	:	Intensive Rural Development Programme
IRRI	:	International Rice Research Institute
ICAR	:	Indian Council of Agricultural Research
JLRO	:	Junior Land Reforms Officer
LLP	:	Low Lift Pump
LRA	:	Land Reforms Act
LRO	:	Land Registry Office
LRS	:	Land Reforms Survey
NAP	:	National Awami Party
NSS	:	National Sample Survey

OB	:	Operation Barga
RLP	:	River Lift Pumps
RS	:	Revenue Survey
STW	:	Shallow Tube Well
TN	:	Ton
TMT	:	Thousand Metric Ton
TSP	:	Trends in Seeds Production
UNDP	:	United National Development Programme
WAPDA	:	Water and Power Development Authority
WBLRA	:	West Bengal Land Reforms Act
WBEAA	:	West Bengal Estate Acquisition Act
WBPKS	:	West Bengal Provincial Kisan Sabha

CHAPTER ONE

Introduction

1.1 THE PROBLEM OF GROWTH AND EQUITY

During the last two decades, some parts of West Bengal and Bangladesh have had an unprecedented growth in agriculture due to the expansion of irrigation facilities and extensive use of high yielding variety (HYV) seeds, fertilizers and pesticides. In West Bengal, the districts which deserve special mention in this context are Burdwan, Hoogli, Nadia and some parts of 24 Parganas. In Bangladesh such agriculturally advanced districts are Comilla, Chittagong, Dinajpur and Kushtia. These areas today constitute the 'green revolution' belts of Bengal[1] (see Map 1). Experiments in these districts in the use of modern inputs have provided a new model for agricultural growth. Attempts are being made to replicate the model in other parts of Bengal. In this study, an attempt has been made to explore the nature of agricultural growth in the green revolution belts and its role in influencing land relations.

The agriculturally advanced districts of West Bengal are mostly located in the alluvial Gangetic delta. An expansion of surface and underground irrigation facilities helped these districts to increase the net cropped area, cropping intensity as well as yield rate. Between 1977 and 1981, the surface water irrigation programme made considerable progress. Major government canals like Kangshabati and Mayurakshi irrigated approximately 20 million acres or 80,000 hectares, an all time high. The Damodar Valley Corporation (DVC) succeeded in supplying water to more than 50 per cent land in Burdwan district alone. More recently, the Teesta Irrigation project opened up a new era in the relatively dry districts of North Bengal. The programmes to tap underground irrigation sources with the use of deep and shallow tubewells (DTW and STW) too helped in increasing the overall irrigation intensity in the state.[2] In the early

---

[1] Here 'Bengal' refers to both West Bengal and Bangladesh as this is convenient to describe many commonalities.

[2] Irrigation intensity is equal to gross irrigated area divided by net irrigated area.

eighties Nadia district registered the highest irrigation intensity of 1.34 due to the spread of ground water irrigation in the early seventies.[3] In 1985-6, the West Bengal Government launched an intensive programme for constructing wells, shallow tubewells, deep tubewells and river lift pumps with the World Bank assistance of US $99 million. Work began in 1988-9 and came to an end in 1994. The programme helped in further growth of irrigation in the state.

Compared with West Bengal, the spread of surface and underground water irrigation programme in Bangladesh has been slow and erratic. So far only one canal irrigation programme, the Ganges Kobadak Project (GKP), has succeeded in irrigating 4,000 hectares in Kushtia and Jessore districts. In other districts, diesel-powered low lift pumps (operated from river banks, *beels* and ponds), DTWs, STWs and various other traditional methods of irrigation increased the irrigation intensity. During the late seventies, Kushtia district had the highest irrigation intensity of 1.37[4] in the country.

The spread of irrigation has been instrumental in influencing the use of HYVs, fertilizers and pesticides both in West Bengal and Bangladesh. Boyce (1987) reported that prior to the seventies the use of chemical fertilizers was quite low: it was only 8.3 kg of nutrient per hectare of gross cropped area in West Bengal in 1965 and 4.6 kg in Bangladesh in 1968. A substantial rise in the use of fertilizer took place in the seventies, reaching 37.3 nutrient-kg per hectare in West Bengal and 28.6 in Bangladesh between 1978 and 1980.[5] The fertilizer intensity (nutrient-kg per hectare per crop) is particularly high in the districts where irrigation intensity is high, e.g. Burdwan, Nadia, Hoogli in West Bengal and Chittagong, Comilla and Kushtia in Bangladesh. Recent surveys have shown further rise in the use of fertilizers.[6]

Like fertilizers, a steady rise in the use of HYVs and pesticides can be noticed in the irrigated areas of West Bengal and Bangladesh. In the (1978-9) period, HYV intensity (percentage area under HYVs) in West Bengal went up to 24.0 in the case of *aman* and 34.4 in the case of *aus*.[7]

[3] Boyce (1987: 165).

[4] Boyce (1987: 167).

[5] Boyce (1987: 177-9).

[6] See also *Economic Reviews*, Government of West Bengal between 1984-5 and 1988-9 for data pertaining to West Bengal and Hossain (1987: 29-30) for data on the fertilizer use in Bangladesh.

[7] Boyce (1987: 180).

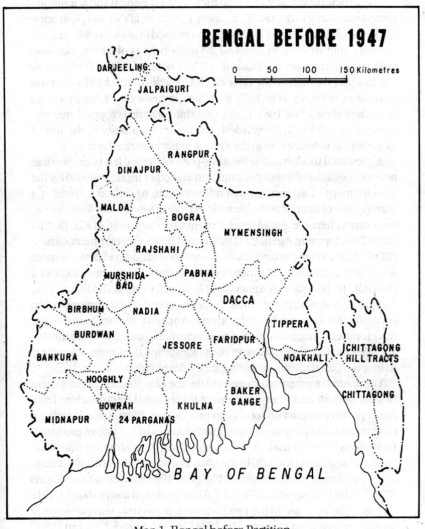

BENGAL BEFORE 1947

0   50   100   150 Kilometres

DARJEELING

JALPAIGURI

RANGPUR

DINAJPUR

MALDA

BOGRA

MYMENSINGH

RAJSHAHI

MURSHIDA-
BAD

PABNA

DACCA

BIRBHUM

NADIA

TIPPERA

BURDWAN

FARIDPUR

CHITTAGONG
HILL TRACTS

JESSORE

BANKURA

NOAKHALI

HOOGHLY

BAKER
GANGE

CHITTAGONG

HOWRAH

KHULNA

MIDNAPUR   24 PARGANAS

BAY OF BENGAL

Map 1. Bengal before Partition.

Entire *boro* cultivation in the state is now carried out with the HYVS and pesticides (see Map 2).

The agriculturally advanced districts in West Bengal show a unique complementarity in the use if irrigation, fertilizers, HYVs and pesticides. In Bangladesh, by 1982-3 HYV seeds were used in about 4 million acres of land under *aman* and *aus,* and 2.3 million acres of land under *boro* cultivation. In a survey, Hossain (1987) noted that the Bangladesh Agricultural Development Council (BADC) distributed 541 thousand pounds of HYV seeds in 1979-80 which increased to 1263 thousand pounds in 1980-1.[8] By 1985, nearly one-third of cereal cropped area was covered by HYVs. In Bangladesh too complementarity in the use of major inputs is noticeable in the agriculturally advanced areas.

Agricultural modernization in some parts of Bengal has been possible not only because of the use of irrigation and other inputs but also for the development of an institutional infrastructure to disburse credit at a nominal rate of interest and to provide extension services. In West Bengal, the Comprehensive Area Development Corporation (CADC), District Rural Development Agencies (DRDA) and Block Development Offices (BDOs) have been particularly active at the village-level development work. In Bangladesh, the Bangladesh Agricultural Development Council (BADC), the Bangladesh Agricultural Research Council (BARC) and the Bangladesh Academy of Rural Development (BARD) attempted to provide the necessary institutional support to the agricultural development programme. Semi-government and non-government agencies too have been active in Bangladesh, and their main objective is to involve Bangladeshis in participatory development.

The spread of irrigation, changes in the use of inputs and development of government and non-government institutional infrastructure have had a positive impact on food crop production. West Bengal's official crop production data show significant changes in the rate of growth of food crops from the mid-sixties, especially in the districts of Burdwan, Nadia, Hoogli and Howrah. In the state as a whole, the official estimate of the production of *aman* rice in 1960 was 4899.5 thousand metric tons (TMT), which increased to 5089.7 TMT in 1969, and then to 6024.0 TMT in 1980. The increase in the production of *boro* crops was particularly significant as it went up from 316.7 TMT in 1969 to 865.2 TMT in 1980.[9]

---

[8] Hossain (1987: 24-5).

[9] Bureau of Applied Economics and Statistics (BAES), Reports on Crop Production Data published between 1960 and 1980.

WEST BENGAL

SIKKIM

BHUTAN

NEPAL

DARJEELING

R. Tista

JALPAIGURI

COOCH BEHAR

ASSAM

0   50   100   150 KMS.

BOUNDARIES:
International .—.—.—.
State ———————
District ....

B   I   H   A   R

WEST
DINAJPUR

MALDA

R. Ganga

BANGLADESH

MURSHIDABAD

BIRBHUM

R. Damodar

PURULIA

BURDWAN

NADIA

BANKURA

HOOGHLY

Calcutta

MIDNAPORE

HOWRAH

TWENTYFOUR
PARGANS

ORISSA

BAY OF BENGAL

Map 2. West Bengal Today.

The net output of wheat, sugarcane and potato also rose in the sixties and seventies. Official data on crop production in Bangladesh too shows a rise in the yield rate of major crops like *aman, aus, boro,* jute and vegetables. The growth of food production has accelerated from about 2.5 per cent a year during 1950-71 to about 2.9 per cent during the1971-85 period. The production of the cereal crop has also increased from about 2.6 per cent a year during 1950-71 to about 3.4 per cent during the 1971-85 period.[10] All these data clearly indicate a new trend in Bengal agriculture, especially in some of its agriculturally prosperous districts. The trend clearly shows the growing popularity of 'new technologies' and the corresponding growth in crop production.[11]

The problem of agricultural growth in Bengal is closely linked with the problem of equity. It has been noticed in many countries that the fruits of development do not reach the poor. Some gain more than the others which, in the long run, widens the gap between the rich and the poor. Several writers have noted such trends in agriculturally advanced regions of Asia.[12] For example, Griffin writes,

In most of the other countries in which high yielding varieties of food grains are being introduced, technical change is heavily biased in favour of some farmers against others. In part this is a result of the biological characteristics of new seeds: they require an abundant and controlled water supply and hence are most suitable for regions which already enjoy a good irrigation system. In part, also, technical change has had a discriminatory impact because the new varieties are intensive in their use of material inputs especially fertiliser and market imperfections restrict the access of small peasants to many factor markets, particularly credit. ... Perhaps the most important reason for the bias of the 'green revolution' is the bias of government policy. For many years research, extension and investment programmes in agriculture have been devoted to raising output (preferably exportable output); their primary concern has not been to increase the welfare of the rural population and improve the distribution of income and wealth. (1973: 52-3)

[10] Hossain (1987: 29-36).

[11] In general, 'new technologies' include irrigation, modern inputs as well as machineries. The development of machineries has not come about in Bengal agriculture the way it did in other green revolution areas in India. In the present context, new technologies would include only irrigation and modern inputs like HYV seeds, fertilizers and pesticides.

[12] For an overview see Bardhan (1970), Ladejinsky (1977).

Beteille (1974) too observed that progressive farmers have become 'ambidextrous', able to manipulate both traditional and modern institutions to their advantage. There is no denying the fact that this has been, by and large, the trend in most developing countries. However, what Griffin and many other writers have not noted about agrarian change under the impact of new technology is that there exist considerable regional differences with regard to the kind of impact that technological growth can make on agrarian structure. State intervention, participation of the poor in poverty alleviation programmes and restructuring of local-level political institutions can go a long way in reaching the goals of social equity. The case of green revolution in Bengal has been examined here from this perspective.

The impact of agricultural growth on agrarian social structure in West Bengal and Bangladesh, especially in the agriculturally advanced regions, are in many ways similar. A rise in the number of agricultural labourers could be noticed in many districts. In West Bengal, landlessness is acute, especially in the green revolution belts. The census figures show a steep rise in the number of agricultural labourers in many areas in the seventies. In 1981, agricultural labourers as a percentage of agricultural workers went up to 25.23 per cent in West Bengal. The percentage was particularly high in districts like Burdwan, Hoogli, Birbhum and Nadia the most fertile areas of the state. In the case of Bangladesh, the percentage was high in Comilla, Chittagong, Dinajpur and Kushtia. The number of landless households increased from 1.5 million in 1951 to 18.75 million in 1977. The percentage of landless labourers went up again between the 1973-4 and 1977 period from 21.4 to 34.7[13] (see Map 3).

In both parts of Bengal the percentage of sharecroppers has remained high. Bandyopadhyay (1993), quoting a survey report of the Government of West Bengal, pointed out that in the early eighties the state had nearly two million *bargadars*. Siddiqui *et al.* (1988) noted that about one-fifth of total agricultural land was under shared tenancy in Bangladesh in the mid-eighties. The advent of green revolution has made the position of the sharecroppers extremely vulnerable. The eviction of unregistered tenants has increased at an alarming rate in Bangladesh. For lack of resources, sharecroppers have not been able to optimize their gains by using modern inputs. Cultivation with the help of hired wage labourers now offers a better scope for profit to the landowners. In this study, an attempt has been made to examine in detail how far the spread of new

[13] Alamgir (1977: 34).

technologies has affected the leasing arrangements and productive efficiency of the tenants.

The growth of agricultural labourers or rural poor as a result of technological change is often described as the process of proletarianization. In a narrow sense, as noted by Tilly (1981), the proletarians are those who receive wages from capitalists for relatively unskilled work performed in large establishments under intense discipline. In the broader sense, it would mean anyone who sells labour power, regardless of the modalities of that sale. The huge labour force in rural Bengal, in this broad sense, can also be described as rural proletarians. Contemporary writers like Tilly (1981) and Standing (1982) have pointed out other attributes. For example, proletarianization would mean certain qualitative changes such as purification of wage relations in which the non-monetary elements of remuneration are progressively suppressed and more wage labourers get cash payment as determined by the market forces and development of consciousness. It is pertinent in this context to note, how far landlessness and rural proletarianization has proceeded in rural Bengal? How can this process be described within a specific theoretical and conceptual framework? What are its repercussions for the society as a whole?

The problem of rural inequalities have prompted actions on the part of the state in both halves of Bengal. It has been pointed out by some writers that state interventions in developing countries have done more harm than good as politicians and bureaucrats use the state resources to their advantage.[14] Thus Grindle and Thomas (1993) noted that citizens use political influence and pressure to get access to benefits allocated by the government; politicians use government resources to hold on to power; public officials trade access to government benefits for personal rewards. The net result of all these is an inefficient and inequitable allocation of resources, general impoverishment and reduced freedom. Downs (1957) drew our attention to how politicians maximize their welfare by selling policies for votes. Therefore, the greater state intervention in the sphere of production in many cases resulted in inefficient production arrangement. In West Bengal and Bangladesh, a series of land reform measures were undertaken to put a ceiling on land holdings, to redistribute surplus land among the poor and to protect tenurial rights of the sharecroppers. In West Bengal, a special programme was adopted to register the names of the *bargadars* which was known

[14] Kohli (1987).

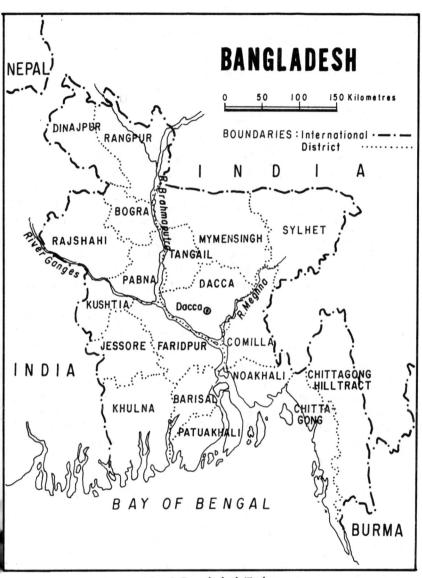

Map 3. Bangladesh Today.

as 'Operation Barga' (OB). In Bangladesh too land reforms ordinance was introduced in 1984 to enforce ceiling provisions and to offer tenurial security to sharecroppers. Have these programmes been successful in solving the problem of inequality? Are they compatible with the basic policies of agricultural growth? These issues have been discussed here.

1.2 AN ALTERNATIVE DEVELOPMENT PARADIGM

The search for an alternative paradigm to explain the problems of development and underdevelopment has assumed special significance in recent times. Modernization theories which dominated the study of development in the Third World laid a great deal of emphasis on the need for total transformation of a traditional society into the types of technology and associated social organizations that characterize the economically advanced and politically stable nations of the West.[15] The theory is based on the assumption that one can describe the general features of both 'traditional' and 'advanced' societies, and 'development' means some kind of transformation from one type into another. Smelser (1963), for example, argued that developed economies are characterized by a highly differentiated structure, and underdeveloped economies lack such differentiation. Therefore, structural differentiation is a *sine qua non* for economic growth in underdeveloped countries. Structural differentiation occurs as more specialized and autonomous units are formed. Economic and social institutions tend to become independent of each other. However, a new process of integration takes place in order to unite differentiated structures. Hoselitz (1960) uses Parsons' well-known 'pattern variables' to develop his differentiation model. For example, he argues that development would involve structural shift from functionally diffused to functionally specific roles. Most modernization theories deal extensively with the internal structural characteristics of developed and developing countries and leave out external factors in economic development. A review of the literature on modernization theory shows a distinct bias in favour of Western type development. It even goes to the extent of equating 'modernity' with 'Western liberal democracies'.

Dependency theories of development, on the other hand,

---

[15] Chief protagonists of the theory are Hoselitz (1960), Moore (1963), Rostow (1953) and Smelser (1963). For a critique of the theory see Amin (1976), Frank (1967), Wallerstein (1979).

comprehend the process and problems of developing countries within the wider socio-historical context of the expansion of European mercantile and industrial capitalism and colonialism. In this paradigm, historically determined external factors account for the development of underdevelopment in the Third World.[16] Therefore, dependency theories deal extensively with the relationships of domination and dependency that exist at various points in the socio-historical process. Thus Baran (1957) argues that advanced industrial nations of the West are fundamentally opposed to the industrialization of the under-developed countries since the latter provide them with raw materials and investment outlets. Frank (1969) maintains that the sectors of an underdeveloped economy are well-integrated in terms of a structure of metropolitan-satellite relationships. Close economic, political, social and cultural ties bind the satellites to each metropolis which expropriates their economic surplus, or a part of it, for its own economic development. The dependency writers, however, opened up an important debate but offered little to explain the economic and social structural peculiarities of the countries in the developing world.

In general, the theory of social and technological dualism shows a process by which the capitalist countries of the West penetrate into the precapitalist agrarian societies of the East, and disintegrate the social and economic system of the later.[17] This kind of penetration results in the development of two sectors, a traditional subsistence agricultural sector and an advanced, dynamic industrial sector. Therefore, side by side with a dominant traditional sector there exists a rapidly growing exchange sector. Dualistic production arrangements are associated with differences in institutional arrangements too. Furthermore, under such conditions inter-sectoral differences in the ownership of wealth would lead to differences in the distribution of political power and political participation.

The chief merit of the theory of economic dualism is that it deals with 'external' and 'internal' factors in economic growth. However, the process of economic modernization in many developing countries has broken the watertight compartmentalization of industrial and agricultural sectors or modern or traditional sectors. In many countries, the two sectors have experienced economic growth or backwardness

[16] The theory has been formulated and developed mainly in the writings of Baran (1957), Frank (1967), Wallerstein (1979).

[17] Lipton (1977).

simultaneously. Sometimes, one sector contributed to the development of the other.

The question that may be raised at this point is that how far these theories are relevant in explaining the problem of growth in the Indian subcontinent? Can it be said that the development processes in the Indian subcontinent are too complex to fit in any of these theoretical models? Besides internal structural factors and external domination and dependence, the development experiences in this region are characterized by a greater role of the state, the local-level political institutions and mass action. The problems of development and underdevelopment in Bengal can probably be better understood within the framework in which one finds a complex interplay of state, institutions and mass actions. The state in post-colonial societies directly appropriates a very large part of the surplus and uses it in the bureaucratic and economic activity. The state, as Alavi (1973) noted, not only consists of bureaucratic-military oligarchy but also politicians and political parties, especially where democratic forms of government operate. Political leadership performs mediatory role between the competing interests of three propertied classes—the domestic bourgeoisie, the metropolitan bourgeoisie and the landowning classes. Universal adult franchise, democratization of political institutions at different levels demand more from the state. It has allowed certain amount of autonomy to the state.[18] Interests of the masses are as important as those of the propertied classes. The state plays a greater role in equations of relations. Political groups and associations have assumed a new role with the changes in the function of the state. There are areas where they find enough room for cooperation with the state. In some cases, as in West Bengal, development programmes have been undertaken and monitored with the help of peasant associations. It is important now to examine how far this kind of involvement of political associations in agricultural development have succeeded in protecting the interest of the poor and what are their short and long term effects. It is also imperative to analyse how far these political bodies have gone to accommodate the demands of the state. In any case, an alternative development paradigm in the case of Bengal has to be examined in the context of changing role of political associations. The functions of the Kisan Sabha in recent times in West Bengal is a case in point. The role of the peasant associations in Bangladesh too merits an investigation.

[18] See Lipton (1991), Poulantzas (1973), Streeten (1993).

In some cases the role of protecting the interests of the rural poor has been taken over by non-political and non-governmental associations, popularly known as the 'NGOs', whose primary objective is to raise the level of consciousness of the 'target people' about their objective conditions of living.[19] It is believed that the awakening of consciousness will have some effect on the relations of domination and subordination. The process of consciouness awakening involves an awareness of two sets of phenomena, an understanding of the politics of objective conditions as experienced by the oppressed and an awareness of power of the oppressor as well as the power of the oppressed. The power of the oppressed would involve perceptions of the notions of solidarity articulated in terms of protection against various forms of oppressions and also realization of what the poor are deprived of in material as well as in psychological terms. The NGO programme is based on the idea that the solidarity among the oppressed is the instrument of change. The difference in the approach of political association and NGOs lies in the fact that the former aims at mobilization as the first step towards development, the latter emphasizes more on the participation.[20] The NGOs in Bangladesh have taken up the task of involving the poor in participatory development. During the last two decades, a large number of NGOs have come into prominence and efforts are being made to channellize government and non-government resources for development through the NGOs.[21] Some of the NGOs in Bangladesh, e.g. the Bangladesh Rural Advancement Committee (BRAC), the Gono Sastha Kendra (GSK), Nijera Kori (NK), Proshika are as active as political groups and associations. Today NGOs have emerged as important local level organizations in all round development in the context of Bangladesh and they are an integral part of an alternative development paradigm.

1.3 A COMPARATIVE STUDY

Sociologists have made use of comparative method in the study of development and underdevelopment for several years. For example,

[19] Freire (1972).

[20] In most cases the process of mobilization presupposes the role of the political party. Political mobilization is considered as the highest level in the process of mobilization.

[21] Many critics of NGO activities in rural India have viewed them as an attempt to frustrate the process of mobilization and rural protests. See Karat (1988).

Moore's (1966) study of some aspects of economic development in China, India and Japan or Wallerstein's (1974) study of 'world system' with the help of comparisons of 'core' and 'peripheral'countries offered useful insights on development trajectories. The method has been used in the study of agrarian movements too. For example, Paige (1975) tests his theory of agrarian unrest with data collected from 70 developing countries. He examined how different ways of organizing agriculture produce different characteristic forms of agrarian unrest. Paige's indepth study of agrarian unrests in Peru, Angola and Vietnam reconfirmed his views on the correlation between agricultural organization and agrarian unrest. Wolf's (1969) study on peasant wars in the twentieth century is also based on comparisons. However, comparative studies of agrarian structure, especially agricultural growth and backwardness are not so common.[22]

One of the obvious advantages of comparative method is that it gives an opportunity to juxtapose cases in order to examine their similarities and differences. As van Schendel (1991) notes, it minimizes the risk of presenting local idiosyncrasies as historical necessities. It helps us to formulate new explanatory hypothesis.[23] It needs to be emphasized that although comparative method had been used by European scholars for many years, its application to the study of societies in South Asia is a recent phenomenon.[24] As a result, tools and methods of comparison of South Asian societies are not as well-developed as one expects them to be.[25] However, the significance of comparative method in the study of South Asian societies cannot be overlooked. The need for comparative studies has become all the more important in South Asian context as these countries shared composite culture and history. The collapse of the colonial rule and Partitions in the subcontinent created new

[22] With the help of comparative studies of agrarian moments in Mexico, Russia, China, Vietnam, Algeria and Cuba, Wolf drew some of his conclusions (1976: 276-302). Scott (1976) too examined the historical development of agrarian society in Lower Burma and Vietnam in a comparative framework.

[23] Schendel (1991: 20-75). See also Ragin (1987).

[24] While conducting micro-level studies on agrarian change and development, some writers have made use of the comparative method. See, for example, Epstein (1962), Schendel (1982).

[25] Some efforts are being made to break the ground under the Indo-Dutch Programme for Alternatives in Development. See, for example, Sengupta (1991), van Schendel (1991).

geographical territories. The newly independent nations followed different strategies for economic development. Comparative studies would offer fresh insights into the positive or negative effects of development programmes.

The Partition of Bengal in 1947 led to the division of the two erstwhile districts of Nadia and Dinajpur. The western part of the Nadia comprising three major subdivisions of Krishnanagar, Ranaghat, Santipur remained with the state of West Bengal in India. The eastern part was carved out to form Kushtia districts in the then East Pakistan. Kushtia town became its headquarters. It included police stations like Mirpur, Meherpur, Khoksa, Kumarkhali (see Maps 4, 5 and 6 for geographical areas of Nadia before the Partition in 1947 and Nadia and Kushtia after the Partition). The undivided Nadia district was bounded by the Ganga in the north and north-east and by the Bhagirathi river on the west. Its adjoining districts were Murshidabad on the north, Burdwan on the west, 24 Parganas on the south and Jessore all along its eastern border. It had an area of 2,898 square miles. Right from the early part of the present century, the district had a fairly developed road, river and railway communication network. Some of the rivers of the district, e.g. the Jalangi and the Garai, were ideal for navigation. The proximity of the district to the old capital Murshidabad and Calcutta city helped the growth of trade in commercial crops. Krishnanagar, Ranaghat, Santipur, Poradaha and Kushtia became important trade centres for rice, jute and vegetables during the late seventeenth century.[26]

The two newly created districts inherited similar infrastructure for agricultural growth. However, the course of events took a new turn with the Partition. Development policies for the agricultural sector in East Pakistan differed considerably from that of West Bengal. During the last forty-five years, a series of measures were undertaken in the two halves of Bengal for improving agricultural conditions. A comparative study of agricultural policies of the two Bengal and their impact on the two districts which used to be one before Partition is one of the main thrusts of the present study. This kind of exercise is likely to throw light on both continuity and change in Bengal agriculture. A comparison of district or block-level data may not be adequate to explain the agrarian problems of Bengal. Village-level data can be used to supplement macro-level findings. In order to do so, two villages, one in Nadia district (Bira) and

[26] See Garrett (1910) for an account of economic infrastructure in the district in the nineteenth and early twentieth century.

the other in Kushtia district (Naopara), were selected for a detailed study. Both these villages were located in the agriculturally prosperous areas of the districts. Bira had an extensive ground water irrigation network, DTWs and STWs helped to increase both irrigation and cropping intensity in the village. The use of modern inputs rose steadily along with the spread of irrigation throughout the seventies and eighties. Naopara village in Kushtia benefited from surface water irrigation projects. The main canal of the Ganges-Kobadak irrigation project ran through the village. Like Bira, Naopara too experienced an increase in irrigation and cropping intensity. The modern inputs too have become popular in the village.

CHAPTER TWO

Agrarian Change in Bengal:
The Late Colonial Phase

2.1 STRUCTURAL CONSTRAINTS

This section deals with the structural constraints to agricultural growth during the later phase of colonial rule, more specifically from the 1920s, and their implications. This background information will help us in following agrarian problems in the post-Independence period. The agrarian conditions in Nadia district as well as in two of its villages have been examined in the next two sections. The years following 1920 are particularly important as most of the data on agricultural situation in Bengal point out some kind of a steady decline.

Let us take a look at the nature of transition in the agrarian economy of Bengal. Till the 1880s Bengal was producing net annual surplus of 1.2 million tons of food grains. However, between 1880 and 1947, a steady impoverishment of agriculture had taken place as per capita output declined considerably.[1] It is important to note that the decline in food output was caused by a significant decline of yields in per unit of land.[2] The sliding trend could be noticed in the official data for the period between 1920 and 1946. During this period, food crops accounted for 70 per cent of the total crop output and an average increase of only 0.7 per cent per year of food crop had an adverse effect on the rural economy. An annual growth of 0.8 per cent in population marginalized 0.7 per cent gain in food crop production.[3] The disparity between the growth of population and food production which started from the twenties widened further in the thirties and forties.[4] A small increase in crop output was possible due to an expansion of acreage under cultivation

[1] Blyn (1966: 96).
[2] Islam (1978: 49-53).
[3] Islam (1978: 53-6).
[4] Islam (1978: 38-40).

between 1920 and 1946, but there was hardly any increase in yield per acre. However, an annual expansion of crop acreage at rate of 0.2 per cent prevented further deterioration in the agricultural sector.[5]

This kind of situation led to the dependence on imported food which continued for quite some time. Data pertaining to trade show that during the 15 years starting 1927-8, imports exceeded exports, and the net import amounted to about 4 per cent of the total domestic supply. According to the Famine Enquiry Commission, up to 1941-2 Bengal had a net import of 1.1 million tons of foodgrains per year which amounted to 1.4 per cent of the domestic supply.[6] Bengal became a net importer of rice from the late twenties. However, the net import was not too substantial to affect the local economy in a normal year. But this kind of condition caused crises at the time of natural disasters like droughts, floods and famines. And as already mentioned, from the early part of the present century, the factor which helped Bengal agriculture to meet the crisis of food shortage was the expansion of crop acreage, primarily due to the reclamation of forest land for cultivation and land classified as 'cultivable waste', 'current fallow' and 'not available for cultivation'. The reclamation process continued throughout the thirties and forties. It was linked with the migration of tribal communities in various parts of the Bengal delta. In order to eke out a living, the migratory labourers cleared forests and made 'uncultivable land' as 'cultivable'.[7] There was a tremendous scope for land reclamation in North and Central Bengal even in the mid-thirties and forties as the 1931 census revealed that 71.2 per cent of total area was cultivable but only 47.7 per cent was actually cultivated. Land reclamation and expansion of crop acreage helped the agricultural sector to pull on in spite of an overall fall in the crop production. Double cropping in some parts of Bengal too was also an important source of acreage expansion. The area under double cropping increased from 44.7 million acres in the early twenties to 57 million acres in the early forties.[8] The spread of irrigation with the inception of the DVC in the mid-thirties led to an increase in the cropping intensity, especially in the central parts of Bengal.

[5] Islam (1978: 69-70). See Bose (1986: 18-33) for an account of land reclamation by tribal migrant labourers in north and central Bengal.

[6] Islam (1978: 110-11).

[7] See Dasgupta (1984), van Schendel and Faraizi (1984) for some aspects of land reclamation by the tribals.

[8] Islam (1978: 70).

Crop production data since the twenties show some important changes in agriculture. Throughout Bengal, the yield of food crop in an acre declined by 0.2 per cent between 1920 and 1946. The drop could be noticed in the divisions like Burdwan, Dhaka and Chittagong, the most fertile areas of Bengal.[9] Only the Presidency division registered a nominal gain of 0.1 per cent annual rate of increase in the yield in food crop in an acre. The drop in the food crop is particularly noticeable during the early forties due to the fall in production of winter and autumn rice in two lean years of 1940/41 and 1942/43.[10]

An examination of official data would show that, in spite of an increase in cropping intensity in some areas, the overall decline in the food crop production took place at the expense of cash crop cultivation. Productivity of cash crop increased at the rate of 1.2 per cent per year between 1920 and 1946. An increase in the productivity of jute accounted for more than 50 per cent of the total increase of non-food crop yield. The regional trends in the yield of other cash crops show an upward trend. In sharp contrast to earlier trends, all the regions had almost identical rates of increase in the yield of cash crops. Rajshahi and Dhaka had the highest area under cash crops, 38 and 39 per cent of the total cultivable land, respectively.[11] The cash crop cultivation did little to improve the economic conditions of the peasantry as the local market for cash crop was unable to withstand the pressure from outside. International demand for raw jute in the early part of the twentieth century led to a substantial rise in the jute prices. Between 1907 and 1913, jute production flourished in most parts of Bengal. However, during the Post-World War I period, high costs for jute production and shrinkage of demand for jute led to a deterioration in the condition of jute growers. The situation went out of control again during World War II when the demand for jute fell again and overall inflationary condition made things worse for the peasantry.[12] A well organized group of traders dictated the terms of trade for jute. Most jute growers sold their product directly to a creditor at a much lower price than the market rate. Moreover, the

[9] According to Blyn (1966), the annual rate of increase in per acre of food crops in Burdwan was -0.3, in Dhaka -0.4 and in Chittagong -0.5. These divisions cover 18, 28 and 13 per cent of cultivable area in Bengal.

[10] See Greenough (1982) for a detailed account on the food crop situation in Bengal during this period.

[11] Blyn (1966).

[12] Bose (1986: 58-69).

problem of storage forced the small growers to sell the product immediately after the harvest.[13] In spite of adverse effects, commercial crop cultivation went on in most parts of Bengal under pressures from traders, *jotedars*, professional moneylenders and moneylenders-cum-landowners.[14]

From the early twenties to the end of forties, hardly any changes could be noticed in the use of farm implements and animal labour.[15] However, with regard to the development of irrigation facilities, some changes came about from the early part of this century. Blyn (1966) showed that in 1905-6, the net irrigated area as a percentage of net sown area was 1.7 which increased to 14.96 in 1920-1 and then to 16.54 in 1945-6 period. The colonial land administrators laid emphasis on the growth of irrigation mainly to ensure cash crop cultivation and food production during the drought periods. The irrigation network did help to reduce the risk to food shortage to some extent during the time of natural disasters. However, it needs to be emphasized that the government investment on irrigation during the early part of the century in Bengal was lower than that of other provinces under the British Raj. The Royal Commission of Agriculture Report (1928) pointed out that irrigation by government canals in the twenties covered only 0.4 per cent of Bengal's net sown area compared to 44.1 per cent in Punjab or 29.7 per cent in Madras. The two major government canals, namely, the Midnapur and the Eden canals irrigated about 1,00,000 acres in Midnapur, Burdwan and Hoogli districts. Later Damodar Canal, which was sanctioned in 1921 to irrigate nearly 2,00,000 acres of rice producing area, succeeded in irrigating an area of 1,34,464 acres extending over 297 villages.[16] Besides these two canals, very little was achieved with regard to the development of irrigation infrastructure in Bengal.

The spread of commercial crop cultivation was not conducive to technological growth in agriculture as it led to diversion of capital from agricultural to non-agricultural sector. Moreover, a higher rate of return from an investment of capital and its use encouraged

[13] van Schendel (1991: 105-7).

[14] Chaudhuri (1975: 150-65).

[15] The quinquential cattle census up to 1930 provided information on ploughs, sugarcane crushers, oil engines, electric pumps and tractors. However, data collected by village panchayats left many gaps (Islam: 1978).

[16] Agricultural Commission Report (1928).

landowners and traders to enter into rural credit market.[17] Investment on credit subsequently diverted capital from agricultural to non-agricultural sector and accelerated the process of land alienation. Thus Chaudhuri (1975) noted that indebtedness caused land transfers on a large scale and it transformed the occupancy tenants into sharecroppers and agricultural labourers. Most land alienation, according to Chaudhuri, was not so much a result of occasional famines, but was the inevitable consequence of rural indebtedness. The fluctuations in the price level and yield rate discouraged large-scale investments in agriculture. The only market that ensured a good and steady return was the credit market.[18] Islam (1978) presented some data on the rate of interest on agricultural loans. Between 1920 and 1946, interest on loans on usufructuary mortgage generally varied from 18.75 to 37.50 per cent per annum. Interests on loans given without security were much higher, sometimes as high as 300 per cent per year.[19] Such a high rate of interest offered a sizeable and steady return of capital to the moneylenders.[20] The spread of commerial crop cultivation, emergence of landowners-cum-money-lenders and traders, and land alienation led to the development of a new kind of cultivation arrangement in which sharecroppers and agricultural labourers came into prominence. Peasants who lost control of their land either by mortgage or through sale were allowed to continue cultivation on a 50 : 50 share basis under the new owners.

Between 1920 and 1945, the number of sharecroppers as well as the area under sharecropping cultivation increased. The Bengal Land Revenue Commission Report stated that in 1938 only 20 per cent of the total cultivated area was under sharecropping arrangement which increased to 25 per cent in 1944. Sharecropping became popular, especially in the forties. There was a marked increase in the percentage of land under sharecropping in a number of districts between 1939-40 and 1946. For example, in Dinajpur it increased from 14.5 to 37.2 per

[17] In this context Bhaduri's (1973) classic account on the interlinkage of landownership and rural credit and its implications for technological change is relevant in understanding the situation.

[18] Chaudhuri (1975: 105-25). See also Chaudhuri (1969), Islam (1978).

[19] Islam (1978: 157-83).

[20] Mukherjee (1957) who compiled Annual Registration Department Reports on land sales and mortgages in Bengal between 1929 and 1943 showed a rising trend in land sales right from the early thrities. He noted significant increase in the number of mortgage sales in the period.

cent, in Jalpaiguri from 25.9 to 50.9 per cent, in Malda from 6 to 30.1 per cent and in Midnapur from 17.1 to 25.2 per cent.[21] Sharecroppers who lacked resources to invest on agricultural production and who encountered the heavy burden of rent and interest were not in a position to raise productivity by using adequate inputs.[22] Therefore, the diversion of capital from agricultural to non-agricultural sector alienated landowner-cum-moneylenders and traders from the process of production; and sharecroppers were unable to raise productivity. Thus, the prospect for agricultural growth during the last phase of colonial rule looked extremely bleak.

Right from the early part of the present century, the number of agriculture labourers too rose in most parts of Bengal. According to a Report on the Condition of Lower Classes of Population in Bengal (also known as Dufferin Report), at the turn of the century around 1888, about 26 per cent of all rural households had 'agricultural labour' as their only or principal occupation while another 13 per cent subsisted on labour as the secondary source of income. Wage labour provided 13 million rural Bengalis with all or part of their livelihood. The highest proportions found in western districts and in one district in South-East Bengal and the lowest was in the north and east.[23] Half a century later, in 1939, the Land Revenue Commission noted that 22 per cent of all rural households were dependent entirely or partially on agricultural wages. Another all-Bengal survey was carried out in 1946-7. The survey which covered 15,000 households throughout Bengal found that 34 per cent of all households were either partially or entirely dependent on wage labour.[24] On the basis of all these findings, one can safely conclude that, by the end of the colonial rule, at least one-fifth of all rural households were dependent on wage labour in some form or the other.

The number of wage labourers in Bengal rose primarily for two reasons. First, migration of tribals, e.g. Santhals and Oraons towards the Gangetic Bengal and non-tribals from other states to Bengal delta led to

[21] Raychaudhuri and Chakraborty (1981: 125).
[22] Ghosh (1987) who examined the nature of productivity under sharecropping and small peasant holdings noted that the small holding peasants did better in raising yield rates during the late colonial period.
[23] Schendel and Faraizi (1984) made an extensive study of the Dufferin Report.
[24] Government of West Bengal (1953).

a rise in the number of labourers. Most of the central districts in Bengal experienced an inflow of migratory population.[25] Second, a steady rise in the rate of growth of population from the beginning of the present century put pressure on land and shrunk the land-man ratio. The percentage increase of population during the 1921-31 period was 7.3 and it went up to 18.2 in 1931-41 (Table 2.1). Such a phenomenal rise in the growth of population in the thirties created further pressure on land. A closer look at the rate of growth of population in the divisions in Bengal right from the 1872 census to the 1931-41 period would show some trends (Table 2.2). The growth rate was consistently high in the divisions like Dhaka and Presidency due to expansion of metropolitan cities where migratory population hoped to find jobs, especially in jute mills and various small-scale industries. The growth was also high in the Rajshahi and Chittagong subdivisions where the scope for land reclamation allured the floating migrant population. In the central part of Bengal, in Burdwan subdivision, the growth was a bit erratic up to 1921, as for the migrants this part of Bengal remained a transit zone since its land was already well-utilized. Not much is known about the inter-division variations in the natural growth of population. There hardly existed any reasons for differential fertility in the divisions. Therefore, the process of migration remained an important variable in explaining the demographic change in the district. Thus, the problem of agricultural backwardness in Bengal from the early part of the present century was directly liked with a number of socio-economic and demographic factors.

TABLE 2.1: VARIATION IN THE POPULATION OF BENGAL SINCE 1901

Census Year	Population in Million	Percentage Increase
1901-11	46.3	—
1911-21	47.5	2.5
1921-31	51.0	7.3
1931-41	60.3	18.2

SOURCE: Census Reports.

[25] van Schendel and Faraizi (1984).

TABLE 2.2: PERCENTAGE VARIATIONS OF POPULATION
IN THE DIVISIONS BETWEEN 1872 AND 1931

Division	1872-81	1881-91	1891-1901	1901-11	1911-21	1921-31
Burdwan	-2.8	+4.0	+7.2	+2.8	-4 9	+7.4
Persidency	+10.5	+3.9	+5.4	+5.1	+0.4	+7.0
Rajshahi	+4.8	+4.7	+6.2	+8.2	+2.0	+2.7
Dhaka	+14.6	+13.0	+9.6	+11.4	+7.1	+8.2
Chittagong	+3.8	+17.4	+13.0	+13.8	+9.9	+13.0
Bengal	+6.7	+7.5	+7.7	+8.0	+2.8	+7.3

SOURCE: Census Reports.

2.2 THE CASE OF NADIA

Early accounts about the agricultural conditions in the Nadia district, especially during the pre-British period, are extremely sketchy (see Map 4). One of the earliest District surveys was conducted by Todar Mal in 1583.[26] At the time of this survey, Bengal was divided into 19 administrative divisions called *sarkars* and Nadia at that time was a part of Satgaon *sarkar*. During Todar Mal's survey, the north-east portion of the present district was carved out and added to Boosnah *sarkar*, and some parts of the south became a part of Selimabad *sarkar*. One of the primary objectives of the survey was to demarcate the district boundary. It dealt very little with the land problems like cropping pattern, productivity, acreage under cultivation and so on.

The other survey reports were not better in terms of providing information on agriculture. The second Mughal settlement of the district was completed in 1658 and it was known as Shah Shujah's settlement. The boundaries were demarcated again during this survey. The number of *sarkars* rose to 34. During the time of Shah Shujah's settlement, the Nadia Raj consolidated its power in the district.[27] Nadia Raj Bhavananda helped Man Singh during his expedition against Pratapaditya in Jessore and was handsomely rewarded for the job. As a result, two of the descendants of Nadia Raj, Gopal and Raghav, became owners of large territory. It was Raghav who moved Nadia Raj's capital from Matiari to Krishnanagar during the late seventeenth century.[28]

Shah Shujah's settlement survey was followed by Murshid Kuli Khan's

[26] Hunter (1875).
[27] Kemm and Pringle (1928: 51-3).
[28] Garrett (1910: 104-5). See also Majumdar (1978) and Siddiqui (1976).

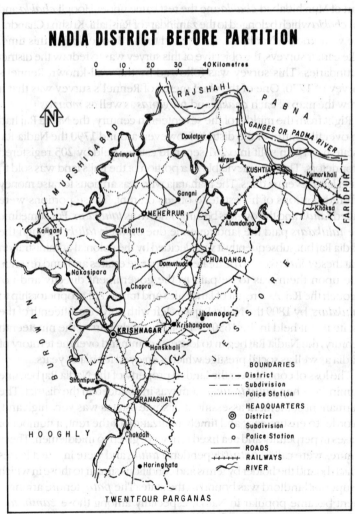

NADIA DISTRICT BEFORE PARTITION

0   10   20   30   40 Kilometres

BOUNDARIES
- · — · — District
- — · · — Subdivision
- ·········· Police Station

HEADQUARTERS
- ◎ District
- ○ Subdivision
- ● Police Station

- ─── ROADS
- ++++++ RAILWAYS
- ∼∼∼ RIVER

Map 4. Nadia District before Partition.

settlement survey which was prepared in 1722. An important administrative reform took place at the time of this survey. Administrative unit *chaklas* replaced the *sarkars*. Two-fifths of Nadia became a part of Murshidabad *chakla* and the rest came under Hoogli *chakla* and Nil *chakla* which belonged to the zamindars of Rajshahi. Krishna Chandra, the well-known Nadia Raj, succeeded to the throne during this time. Like earlier surveys, the objective of this survey was to redraw the district boundaries. This survey was followed by the well-known Rennel's survey of 1770. One of the chief merits of Rennel's survey was that it drew the map of each *chakla* and *parganas* as well as *mouzas*.

Right from the middle of the seventeenth century, the Nadia Raj had an overall control of the district. However, around 1790 the Nadia Raj estate had been split into 261 separate estates held by 205 registered proprietors. This was inevitable as a portion of the Raj's land was sold to meet land revenue dues. The maharaja who was anxious to raise money offered portions of his estate to others on rent. These portions were called *taluks* and the owners became known as *talukdars*. For sometime the *talukdars* paid the land revenue due on their *taluks* through the Nadia Raj but subsequently it was decided by the colonial administration that these *taluks* were to be treated as separate estates and land revenue due upon them was to be paid to the government directly and not through the Raj. As a result of land sales and transfer of proprietorship to *talukdars*, by 1809 the Nadia Raj was left with only one-fifteenth of the estate that it held in the 1650s.[29] From the early part of the nineteenth century, the Nadia Raj began to loose its command over the territory of Nadia as well as social prestige which it enjoyed for many years.

The loss of control over the landed property of the Nadia Raj became imminent when *patni taluk* system was introduced in the district. The permanent settlement assessment of some estates was very high and, in order to ensure easy and timely realization of the rent, a number of leases in perpetuity and at a fixed rent were given to middlemen. These tenures were called *patni* (dependent) *taluks* and were in effect leases which bound the holder by terms and conditions similar to those in which a superior landlord was bound to the state. The *patni* tenure arrangement became popular in Nadia, especially among those *zamindars* who wanted to stay away from the actual management of their estate. Undertenure of the *patnidars* were called *darpatnis* and those created by the *darpatnidars* were known as *sepatni*. These undertenures

---

[29] Garrett (1910).

enjoyed permanent, transferable and heritable rights and had the same privileges and responsibilities as the superior tenures.[30] In this way, the colonial land tenure policies led to a new kind of hierarchical arrangement in the landholding structure in Nadia.

This kind of structuring of landholding rights, or what is known as the process of 'subinfeudation', was an unique feature of land tenure system in Nadia since the mid-nineteenth century. It was also linked with a special kind of tenurial arrangement, locally known as *utbandi* system. During the first two decades of the present century, about two-third of the cultivable land came under the *utbandi* tenurial arrangement in the district. *Utbandi* literally meant an assessment of rent according to cultivation. Under this arrangement, the rent was also determined by an appraisement of the crop on the ground and was paid in crop too. This was a special form of tenancy which went on from year to year and sometimes from season to season. Because of its short duration, the Bengal Tenancy Act of 1885 offered no occupancy rights to *utbandi* tenants.[31] Lack of tenurial security and arbitrary assessment of rent at times resulted in extreme hardship to the tenants and adversely affected agricultural productivity.

The earlier survey accounts dealt very little with the condition of rural labourers in Nadia although they comprised a sizeable percentage of rural population. Hunter (1875), who presented an account of the occupational structure of the inhabitants of Nadia, recorded 44.74 per cent as tenant-cultivators and 18.61 as labourers in the district (Table 2.3). Hunter noted that the emergence of agricultural labourers was a mid-nineteenth century phenomenon. The migration of semi-Hinduized population from neighbouring districts accounted for the rise in the number of labourers. Hunter's account made it clear that nearly two-third of the district population comprised tenant cultivators and labourers. In spite of this, the official surveys in later years, e.g. Garett

[30] Pringle and Kemm (1928).

[31] Only after twelve years of occupation, occupancy rights were offered under Tenancy Act of 1885. See Kemm and Pringle (1928: 64). The Rent Act classified *ryots* into three groups, (1) *mukararidars* or *istanraridars* who cultivated land at fixed rate since the time of the Permanent Settlement or the *ryots* from whom rents have not been changed for 20 years, (2) occupancy *ryots* who had cultivated land for an uninterrupted period of 12 years and (3) non-occupancy *ryots* who were enable to prove 12 years of continuous possession of land.

TABLE 2.3: OCCUPATIONAL PATTERN (*in percentage*)
OF POPULATION IN NADIA, 1872

Occupation	Percentage
Public servants	1.08
Professionals	2.26
Zamindars	0.72
Servants of Zamindars	0.04
High level Transport Workers	0.03
Moneylenders and Merchants	0.78
Clerks	0.62
Tenant Cultivators	44.74
Artisans	2.59
Weavers	2.55
Manufacturers	0.02
Construction Workers	1.92
Petty Traders	1.98
Dealers	10.85
Personal Service Personnel	4.55
Labourers	18.61
Animal handlers	1.15
Lowland Transport Workers	2.75
Unemployed	1.90
Others	0.86
Total	100.00

SOURCE: Hunter (1875).

(1910), Pringle and Kemm (1928), commented in a cursory manner about the condition of rural labourers in the district. As a result, the rural labourers of Nadia remained 'the people without history' (see Map 5).[32]

In spite of the emergence of hierarchical land holding structure, and rise in the number of tenant cultivators and labourers, the agricultural economy of the district showed sings of improvement in the early part of the present century. Pringle and Kemm in their Settlement Survey Report (1928) noted that in the 1920s Nadia was self-sufficient in producing rice. There was a surplus of 4.3 per cent of the food crops in the district and it produced enough rabi crops.[33] As much as 32 per cent of the total area of the district was covered under *rabi*. In comparison

[32] See van Schendel and Faraizi (1984).
[33] Pringle and Kemm (1928: 28-30).

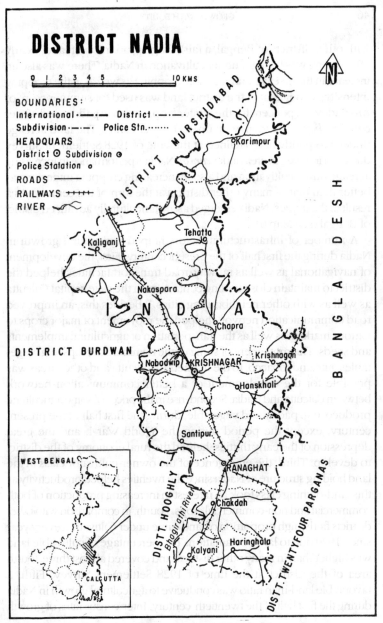

Map 5. Nadia District after Partition.

with other districts of Bengal, a fairly large proportion of land, nearly 70 per cent, was brought under cultivation in Nadia. There was also an increase in the acreage under double cropping as well as in the cropping intensity; 59 per cent of the district land was used for summer crop, or *aus* paddy, 32 per cent for the winter crop, or *aman* paddy, and 49 per cent for *boro*. The total went up to 140 per cent.[34] The land acreage under *aus* paddy had declined at the time of 1928 Settlement Survey due to an increase in area under *aman*. Nadia's performance in increasing acreage under cultivation and also in increasing cropping intensity was better than that of many other districts at the turn of the century. As a result in the thirties, Nadia emerged as an agriculturally advanced district of Bengal (see Map 6).

A number of infrastructural factors helped agricultural growth in Nadia during the first half of the present century. First, the development of navigational as well as railway/road transport facilities helped the district to maintain close trading contacts with the state capital Calcutta as well as with other neighbouring cities.[35] Besides this, an improved road communication network helped the movement of major crops to various markets as well as the transportation of agricultural implements and seeds. The movement of some of the commercial crops, e.g. vegetables, jute and tobacco, to the markets in Calcutta and other areas was possible for the development of a better communication network between Calcutta and Nadia. Second, rise in the prices of some agricultural produce, e.g. paddy and vegetable, during the first half of the present century, except the period during the World War I, and the great depression of the early thirties, helped the rural economy of the district to develop. Third, the emergence of the owner-cultivator class in the land holding structure of Nadia since the twenties helped productivity as this land-owning class took an interest in increasing production of both commercial and non-commercial crops. Fourth, in comparison with other districts fairly high proportion of land came under cultivation every year since 1920 due to land reclamation. The percentage of cultivable land was higher than in many other districts and covered almost three-fourth area of the district at the time of 1928 Settlement Survey. Fifth, a favourable land-man ratio was conducive to agricultural growth in Nadia during the first half of the twentieth century. Inter-census rates of growth

[34] Ibid. (1928: 30).
[35] The river Jalangi provided navigational opportunities with other commercial areas.

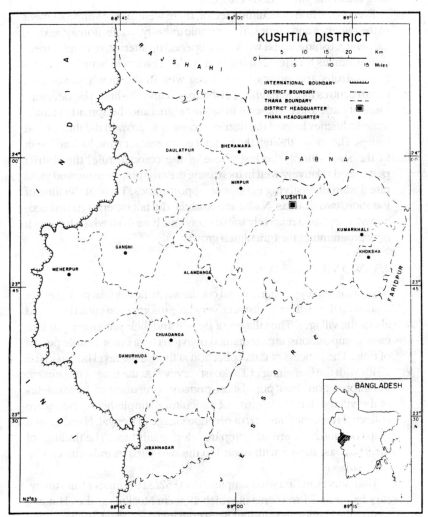

Map 6. Kushtia District after Partition.

of rural population remained below the state average, except for the 1911-21 period. This was also true of the eastern part of the district or area under the jurisdiction of Kushtia.[36]

Even in the non-agricultural sector, there were signs of improvement in the twenties and thirties. The ceramic industry, confectionary, textile, carpentry, fishing, metal work, etc., opened up alternative employment opportunities for the inhabitants of Nadia. Traders in betal leaf, vegetables, fruits and pulses were doing well in the newly developed urban centres like Ranaghat, Krishnanagar and Kushtia. The development of trade and commerce in urban centres and the spread of small-scale industries helped the district economy to grow in the thirties and forties. Therefore, though the general economic scenario looked bleak in the state during the last phase of the colonial rule, the district performed relatively well in increasing the cropping acreage and yield rate and in diversifying economic opportunities. Thus, at the time of Partition, two districts, Nadia and Kushtia, did not inherit a ruined economy. They had a relatively stable economic base from which to launch new programmes for agricultural growth.

2.3 TWO VILLAGES

Most of the surveys on agricultural conditions in the colonial period either dealt with the state or its districts; very little information could be found about the villages. The villages of Bengal and their settlement pattern, caste compositions, etc., remained oblivious for a considerable period of time. The process of data collection at the village level began in the 1840s with the launching of Thakbast survey.[37] At the time of the survey, the information about population, primary occupation of the residents of the village, land types, use of agricultural implements, etc., were collected from each *mouza* or revenue village in Bengal. Hand-drawn maps of *mouzas* were also prepared during this time. The findings of the Thakbast survey with regard to the two villages in Nadia can be summarized.

Thak survey in Bira was completed in 1852. At the time of this survey, Bira had only 74 residents of which 49 were Muslims and 25 Hindus. Most of the Hindus and Muslims were primarily dependent on agriculture.

---

[36] Boyce (1987: 139-40). See also Boyce (1989).

[37] Thak survey records, mostly hand written, are available in the District Record Rooms in Krishnanagar and Kushtia.

Some had subsidiary occupations like fishing, carpentary and weaving. The village had a total of 386 acres of land. The Thak map of the village gave us an idea about the residential pattern. No segregation could be noticed among the Hindu and Muslim households. Most of the houses were located on the south-western part of the village (see Map 7). The main objective of the Thak survey was to demarcate boundaries of each *mouza* and to collect demographic data and information about the use of agricultural implements. Nothing could be found about the cropping pattern, yield rate or land tenure arrangement.

The Thak survey report for village Naopara was completed in 1855. At the time of the survey, the village had a total population of 185, of which 115 were Muslims and the rest were Hindus. The village had a total area of 507 acres. In this village too no residential segregation could be noticed among the Hindu and Muslim households (see Map 8). Most of the households were located on the south-western part of the village. A tributary of the Garai river known as Maragarai was flowing on the western part of the village.

In 1890, an attempt was made again to collect village-level data systematically. The Government of Bengal carried out the Cadestral Survey (CS) to collect data from each village about the land-ownership, the nature of intermediary holdings, the number of *raiyats*, the revenue payable to the government, the crops grown and the cropping intensity. The CS began in 1890 in Chittagong and ended in 1940 in Dinajpur. The survey was carried out from the south-east to the north-west. Information were collected about each plot in a *mouza*, and a map of the village was also prepared.[38] Each CS Report contained the names of the *zamindars*, *raiyats*, intermediaries and tenants. The CS data provide us an opportunity to comment on the landholding structure, cropping pattern and cropping intensity in each village at the time of the survey. The CS reports for Bira and Naopara were completed in 1935. Both villages had an extremely hierarchical landholding pattern.[39] For instance, Naopara had altogether 13 *zamindars*, and nearly two-third of the village land was owned by 5 *zamindars*. It also had a large number of occupancy tenants, e.g. *raiyats, korfas, basat praja, paricharak,*

[38] Schendel (1982: 33-5).

[39] Prior to CS, most of the land in the village belonged to the Cossim Bazar Raj Land transfer from the hands of the Cossim Bazar Raj to others took place from 1900. See Nandy (1986) for more details.

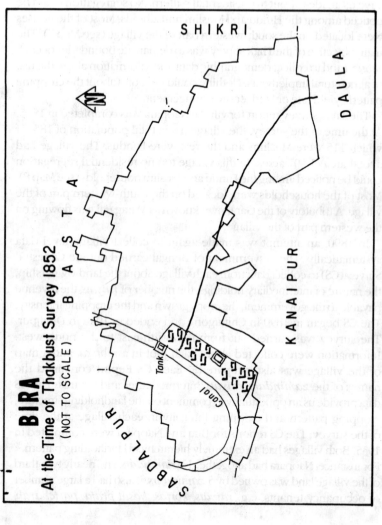

Map 7. Bira Thak Survey Map.

chandina. There were as many as 425 *raiyats* and 144 *korfas.*[40]

Because of its relatively larger size, at the time of CS, Naopara *mouza* was divided into two parts; the sourthern part came to be known as Naopara and the northern part as Krishnapur. The links between these two parts were severed for all practical purposes since the survey. The distant location of households eventually led to the growth of two villages, Naopara and Krishnapur. Naopara, which had an area of 385.45 acres, was chosen for the present study. Right from the time of CS three-fourth of land in the village was cultivable and the rest was used for roads, offices, schools. Homesteads, tanks and gardens too occupied some of the land. The cultivable land was used mostly for production of only one crop, either *aus* or *aman* paddy. The yield rate of *aman* varied between 10 and 16 *maunds* and that of *aus* between 8 and 10 *maunds* per *bigha.* Rain-fed low lying land of the village was ideally suited for the cultivation of *aman* and the high land for the cultivation of *aus.*

The agricultural conditions in the village Naopara were better at the time of CS, both in terms of acreage and productivity. Agro-climatic conditions and natural fertility of the soil helped agricultural growth in the village. A better communication network too helped agricultural advancement. Navigational facilities through the Garai river and its tributaries and transportation along metallic roads opened up an access for agricultural produce to markets in nearby cities and towns. Railway links through Mirpur (a railway station located 5 km away) to other areas facilitated transportation of crops.

At the time of CS, the land holding structure of Bira too was extremely hierarchical. There were as many as 18 *zamindars* at the top of the hierarchy, most of whom resided either in the nearby town of Ranaghat or in Calcutta. The CS report recorded the names of as many as 89 *patnidars*, 120 *darpatnidars* and nearly 200 occupancy tenants. Nearly 90 per cent village land was under cultivation. The cultivable land was used for producing either *aus* or *aman.* The high land in Bira was particularly suitable for the cultivation of *aus* and jute. The proximity of the village to Calcutta city and access of village produce to Calcutta trade markets helped the process of commercialization from the thirties.

The CS records were revised in West Bengal and East Pakistan after 1947. In West Bengal, it was revised in accordance with the West Bengal

---

[40] *Raiyats* were occupancy tenants, *korfas* had less tenurial rights. Generally, those who had less than 10 years of contract for cultivation were called *korfas.*

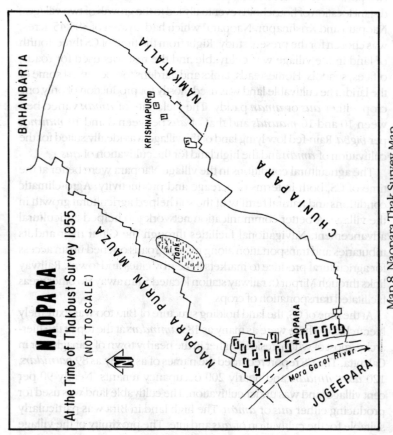

Map 8. Naopara Thak Survey Map.

Estate Acquisition Act of 1954. The survey was called as 'Revenue Survey'. This was the last official survey on the *zamindari* land tenure arrangement in the village. Like CS, RS reports too included the names of *zamindars, patnidars, darpatnidars* and occupancy tenants. The RS reports recorded the names of 19 *zamindars* of Bira, 9 of whom lived in Santipur, one each in Burdwan, Kaliganj, Matiari, Aranghata, Krishnanagar and Ranaghat. The residences of four other *zamindars* were not stated. Between CS and RS surveys, the number of *zamindars* increased from 19 to 29. It confirmed the tendency among the *zamindars* to dispose off their landed property. Auctioning of land due to the inability of the *zamindars* to pay rent could be another possibility. It also showed that the problem of absenteeism in land-ownership was acute. The RS reports also noted a rise in the number of occupancy tenants and diversification in crop production. Cash crop cultivation like jute, sugarcane and tobacco became popular in Bira.

The CS records were revised in East Pakistan in line with the State Acquisition Act of 1955 and the survey was called 'SA Survey' (SAS). The data relating to land holding structure in Naopara at the time of SAS was extremely incoherent. No information is available on the intermediaries, occupancy tenants. At the time of SAS, data was collected on a reporting basis. As a result, inconsistencies crept into the report. A tendency towards over-reporting of landownership was common as many had staked claim on the lands deserted by the Hindu *zamindars*. No information is available in the report about the acreage under cultivation and cropping pattern. Therefore, as far as Naopara village is concerned, the last authentic account on the *zamindari* land-ownership can be found in the Cadestral Survey reports.

Throughout the thirties and forties, changes in the agrarian conditions in the two villages came about gradually. However, the Partition in 1947 brought about sudden ruptures in the agrarian structure, especially in Bira. Thousands of Hindu migrants poured in from various parts of East Bengal into Nadia and other bordering districts of West Bengal.[41] The Namasudra migrants from Kushtia and Jessore found their way into Bira. The arrival of the refugees shrunk the existing land-man ratio in the

[41] The Government of West Bengal carried out a survey in 1950 on the displaced persons from East Pakistan (those who arrived before 1950). The survey showed that the refugees from Jessore, Khulna, Faridpur, Dacca, Pabra, Noakhali and Kushtia settled down in Nadia in large numbers. See Pakrashi (1971).

village. Land transfers took place from the hands of the early settlers to the migrants. The refugees brought with them the knowledge of crop production and entrepreneurship. During the post-Partition period, the refugee farmers began to play an important role in the agrarian transformation in Bira.

Although the nature of agrarian hierarchy in Nadia and its two villages was not different from other parts of Central and South Bengal, infrastructural conditions, the process of land reclamation and agro-climatic factors helped the agricultural growth. Land-man ratio in the district as well as in the villages was also favourable for agricultural progress. Moreover, geographical location of the district, especially its access to trade markets in Calcutta and other town accelerated the process of commercialization of agriculture. With the Partition in 1947, agrarian conditions began to change rapidly both in Nadia and Kushtia. Some of the changes came about as a result of policies adopted by the states. In the next chapter, state policies in shaping agrarian conditions in West Bengal have been taken up for discussion. An attempt has been made to explain how local-level initiatives have influenced agricultural growth. District and village level data have been used to examine some contentious issues. This is followed by a study of agrarian situation in Bangladesh with the help of data collected in Kushtia and one of its villages.

CHAPTER THREE

West Bengal: The New Technology and Agrarian Change

3.1 LAND REFORMS AND LAND RELATIONS

General discontent with the colonial land policy and widespread agrarian unrest in the late forties provoked rethinking on the land tenure arrangement in Bengal. In West Bengal, immediately after Independence two major Acts came into effect to abolish the *zamindari* land tenure system, namely, West Bengal Estate Acquisition Act (EAA) of 1954 and West Bengal Land Reforms Act (LRA) of 1955.[1] Broadly the EAA and LRA had the following objectives:

(a) to abolish *zamindari* and all kinds of intermediary rights in land through acquisition of estates and by paying compensation,

(b) to implement ceiling in land holding,

(c) to discover surplus lands and to redistribute these lands among the poor peasants,

(d) to protect the tenurial rights of the sharecroppers, and

(e) to bring the *raiyats* under the direct control of the state.

Attempts were made to plug loopholes in these Acts by introducing suitable amendments from time to time. For instance, the provisions relating to the ceilings on the holdings were amended in 1965 in order to avoid ambiguities and to stop evasion of land ceilings. Provisions relating to tenurial rights were amended in 1974 to put an end to large-scale evictions. In 1975, an amendment was introduced for the acquisition of homestead lands. More changes were introduced through the West Bengal Landholding Revenue Act of 1979 and the Revenue Rules of

---

[1] Prior to this, the Bargadari Act of 1950 was adopted in order to protect the tenurial rights of the *bargadars*. The LRA of 1956, however, included most of the provisions of the Bargadari Act of 1950.

1980. The 1979 Act put the responsibility of disproving a claim to *bargadari* rights on the land-owners.[2]

In fact, between 1956 and 1969, several amendments were introduced to bring about changes in tenancy relations. For example, it was pointed out that land-owners would receive half of the gross produce in all those cases when they supplied plough, cattle, manure and seed. The place of threshing would be mutually decided by the *bargadar* and the land-owners. The land-owners were allowed to terminate a *barga* when the land cultivated by the *bargadar* and the land under his personal cultivation did not exceed two-thirds of the total land ceiling. These amendments were not enough to plug loopholes in the Land Reforms Act. The eviction cases of sharecroppers were on the rise. Furthermore, the West Bengal Land Reforms (Amendment) Act of 1971 raised the *bargadar's* share to 75 per cent when he supplied all the inputs and the land-owner was entitled to only 25 per cent (50 per cent when all the inputs except labour were supplied by him). The *bargadars* enjoyed the right to receive a receipt from the land-owners upon delivery of the produce to the latter, they also had the right to decide the place of threshing. The *bargadar's* right to cultivation became hereditary. It was made clear that the resumption of land for self-cultivation by the land-owner was permissible only if the land in question together with the other land under his personal cultivation did not exceed 3.0351 hectares and left at least 0.8094 hectares with the *bargadar*.

Although most of the land reforms legislations were enacted in the state right from the fifties, very little was done to implement them. Changes in the implementation of land reforms programme began to take place when the United Front Government assumed office in 1967. Land reforms received top priority. However, the United Front was in power for a short time and, as a result, not in a position to do much.[3] Later on, with the emergence of the Left Front in state politics in 1977, land reforms programmes received attention once again. Land reforms programme of the Left Front included, among other things, relief to peasants by writing off outstanding loan and by providing fresh credit on nominal interest and on easy terms of repayment, exemption of rent of

[2] There were other major amendments with regard to tenurial rights. For example, in 1956, provisions for Bhachash Board was added. In 1956, rules were amended regarding the transfer of rights.

[3] For an account of land reforms programme of the United Front, see Konar (1976 and 1977).

all land-owners owing up to four acres of irrigated land and six acres of non-irrigated land, and fixation of wage for the agricultural landless labourers. As mentioned earlier, the tenancy reforms programme received utmost priority.

Broadly, land reforms programme in West Bengal influenced land-ownership and land relations in three ways. Firstly, the ceiling provisions had a far-reaching effect on the size of holding. Secondly, tenancy reforms programme influenced the position of the lessers and the lessees in a substantial way. And finally, the reforms programme made an impact on the living conditions of the agricultural labourers. Let us first examine the impact on the size of holding.

Land ceilings under the EA Act were fixed as 25 acres of agricultural land and 20 acres of non-agricultural land per family. No ceiling was imposed on land under tank fisheries, orchards, land held by institutions established exclusively for religious and charitable purposes and forests. But land ceilings did very little to change the land holding structure in the fifties and sixties for rampant evasion of ceilings. Various methods were adopted to evade ceiling provisions. For example, agricultural lands with some fruit bearing trees were classified as 'orchards', land located near a tea garden was recorded as 'tea gardens' and land adjacent to a rice mill was classified as 'rice mill'. Almost all the low lying land was converted into 'tank fisheries'. One more novel method was discovered to increase one's holding. Many families claimed that they were governed by the *mitakshara* school of Hindu inheritance law under which a male member of the family became a coparcener of the family property since his birth and could claim partition of the family property even during the lifetime of the father or the head of the household. But for centuries, majority of the Hindu families in Bengal had adhered to the *dayabhag* system of inheritance under which there existed no coparcenary between a man and his sons. In other words, it did not allow the sons to have a share of the property during the lifetime of their father. By declaring adherence to the *mistakshara* school of inheritance, land was kept under the name of each member of the family.[4]

As a result of large-scale evasions of land ceiling legislations, very little was achieved for about one and a half decades to implement the perceptible changes in the land holding structure. Peasant movements in various parts of West Bengal during the late sixties for the seizure of

[4] For an historical account of inheritance rights in Bengal see Illiopolou (1994).

surplus lands helped the then United Front Government to discover *benami* (illegally owned) land. Mitter (1977) showed how in the southern part of 24 Parganas district, the peasants of Sonarpur Police Station took possesion of about 20,000 bighas of *benami* land of the *jotedars*. The peasants forcibly occupied arable land recorded by *jotedars* as fisheries or flooded by them with salt water after evicting sharecroppers as well as arable land left fallow so that sharecroppers had not claimed any right on such land. The movement also helped to take possession of *char* land (the new alluvial formation) and government *khas* land (vested) that the *jotedars* in collusion with the JLRO had recorded as their own.[5] In Burdwan, between 1967 and 1969, when the land grab movement was at its peak, the peasant unions discovered 4448.02 acres of land.[6] The movement succeeded in setting a new trend in land relations in West Bengal. The evasion of land ceiling provisions by the land-owners had stopped. Dasgupta explained its impact in the following words:

During the brief United Front rule by the left-wing parties in 1967 and 1969-70, the village-level committees of poor peasants and landless labourers helped to identify such benami land (that is land held illegally in excess of the permitted limit), took over 300,000 acres of such land and distributed it among the landless. While the legality of such action was disputable there was no denying the effectiveness of bringing about a change to the land relations in rural West Bengal. The beneficiaries of such populist land reform formed the hard core of the support which the Left Front received during the 1977 and 1982 elections'. (1982b:13)

There remains little doubt that the movement contributed a great deal towards initiating dialogues on land ceiling provisions.

New legislations regarding landholding were enacted in 1972 by which a single adult person was entitled to 6.2 acres of irrigated and 8.6 acres of non-irrigated agricultural land. For a family of up to 5 members, the ceiling was 12.4 acres of irrigated and 17.3 acres of unirrigated agricultural land. For a family of more than 5 members, an additional 1.2 acres of irrigated and 1.7 acres of unirrigated land subject to a maximum of 17.3 acres of irrigated and 24.3 acres of unirrigated land holdings were allowed. The strict enforcement of land ceiling legislation and redistribution of

---

[5] See Mitter (1977: 40-75) for some backround information on the movement and for a case study in south 24 Parganas.

[6] See Dasgupta (1987: 58-79), for land grab movement in Burdwan in the late sixties.

surplus land led to an increase of 'marginal groups' (those owning less than one hectare) in the land holding structure. The number of marginal farmers rose from 2.5 million in 1970-1 to 3.5 million in 1976 and then on to 4.1 million in 1980-1. Data provided by the agricultural census operations since 1970 not only showed this kind of trend in land-ownership in West Bengal but also made it clear that the new beneficiaries of land reforms or the receipients of distributed land accounted for the growth of about three-fourth of the additional household in the marginal group. Census figures and official surveys on the land holding structure showed a clear trend towards the emergence of small farmers in the early seventies (Table 3.1). Small farmers were growing in numbers and increasing their share of the operated area. In the early eighties, small farms outnumbered all other types of holdings in West Bengal. The interest of the small farmers were protected by exempting them from paying the revenue in irrigated (those owing less than three acres) and unirrigated (those owing less than six acres) land.

A number of surveys on agricultural growth in India and Bangladesh show that the key players in ushering change in the economy are the small and marginal farmers. In many areas despite worsening policy impact the small producers have been trying to increase their output. They are the principal buyers of modern agricultural inputs. They also produce bulk of the raw materials for export. According to Hossain (1993), the number of small and marginal farmers households in Bangladesh has increased from 6 million in 1960 to 12 to 13 million in

TABLE 3.1: PERCENTAGE DISTRIBUTION OF NUMBER OF HOLDINGS (H) AND AREA UNDER SIZE CLASS (A) IN WEST BENGAL, 1951 AND 1971

| Size Class | 1951 | | 1971 | |
(in acres)	H	A	H	A
0-5	70.67	32.32	82.20	47.25
5.01-10.00	21.21	30.19	13.33	28.94
10.01-02.00	6.63	23.29	4.38	19.25
25.01 and above	1.49	14.20	0.09	4.56
Total	100.00	100.00	100.00	100.00

SOURCES: Census (1951).
        Socio-economic Evaluation Branch Report (1975).
        Government of West Bengal.

1991.[7] Land reforms and state supports programme in West Bengal have offered sufficient incentive to this group. This has not been the case with Bangladesh although the small and marginal farmers there proved their resilience against adverse conditions by producing more per acre than the large farms.

With regard to the protection of the rights of the tenants, land reforms programme had much to offer. Initially when the LRA was adopted, a land-owner was permitted to evict a sharecropper when the land was needed for 'personal cultivation'. Eviction of sharecroppers was a common phenomenon in rural Bengal in the fifties and sixties. The Land Reforms Amendment Act of 1971 attempted to stop misuse of provisions relating to 'personal cultivation'. According to the Amendment Act, the land-owner who terminates the cultivation of *barga* land on the ground of personal cultivation either by himself or by any member of the family will be required under the provision of the Act to live near the land for the most part of the year. Moreover, the main source of earning of the same land-owner must be from agriculture. According to the Amendment Act, when a *bargardar* is evicted from the barga land on the ground of personal cultivation, the same land will have to be cultivated either by the land-owner himself or by the members of his family. Under no circumstances the land-owners will be allowed to cultivate the same land with the help of wage labourers.

Legislative measures were not enough to improve the living conditions of the sharecroppers. It was necessary to give them tenurial rights by some other methods. In order to do so, the Government of West Bengal came out with a new method for the registration of the names of sharecroppeers. The programme came to be known as 'operation barga' (OB). The registration of names was carried out with the help of government workers, *panchayat* members and peasant organizations. The following steps were taken in this operation. First, identification of priority areas with larger concentration of *bargadars*; second, formation of official squads for moving into these priority pockets; third, conducting the meeting of the squad with the *bargadars* and owners preferably in the evening and in a public place; fourth, hearing both the parties by the government officials and examining documents and finally, passing judgement and issuing the certificates to the *bargadars* whose names were recorded.[8]

[7] See Hossain (1993).
[8] Ghosh (1981).

The OB helped to register names of about seven lakh *bargadars* during the late seventies.[9] The number increased steadily till the mid-eighties. A comparison of recording between 1979 and 1980 and between 1980 and 1985 shows that though the percentage slowed down a bit during the second period, spectacular success was achieved during the first period of recording.[10] However, inter-district variations are worth noticing in the recording of *bargadari* rights (Table 3.2). Districts like Midnapur, 24 Parganas, Bankura and Birbhum achieved considerable progress during the first as well as the second period. But districts like Murshidabad and Hoogli succeeded marginally in recording the names of sharecroppers during the second period.

It is true that the primary objectives of *barga* recording was to offer tenurial security. However, attempts were made to enthuse the sharecroppers to use modern agricultural inputs, HYV seeds, irrigation, etc., by offering them loans from banks and cooperatives. How far the programme succeeded in offering security and improving productivity has been discussed in detail in Section 3.4. It is important to examine these questions at length as for the first time a new experiment was carried out in a state on a massive scale to improve the conditions of sharecroppers. One novel feature of the experiment is that it relied entirely on group action by involving the government officials, elected *panchayat* members and kisan sabha activists. Besides the question of improving productivity under OB, several other issues merit close attention, e.g. their social conditions, development of political awareness, etc. Some writers have pointed out that the *barga* recording has not improved the economic conditions of *bargadars*.[11] The recorded *bargadars* have not been using modern inputs and institutional loans have failed to reach the needy sharecroppers. The programme failed to weaken the grip of the rich land-owners. Non-recording of names of a large number of sharecroppers also questions its effectiveness. Some writers draw our attention to the fact that instead of abolishing tenurial relations, the West Bengal Government through this programme has legitimized an age-old practice of exploitation through rent. We shall return to these issues in Section 3.3. The reason for doing so is that some of these points can be examined only with the help of empirical data.

Legislative measures had very little to offer to the landless agricultural

[9] Bandyopadhyay (1979: 4).
[10] Bandyopadhyay (1979), Dasgupta (1984).
[11] Chattopadhyay (1984), Khasnobis (1981), Rudra (1981).

TABLE 3.2: REGISTRATION OF *BARGADARS* UNDER OB, 1979, 1980 AND 1985

District covered	No. of *Mouzas*	No. of *Bargadars* recorded till April 1979	No. of *Bargadars* recorded till April 1980	Percentage increase	No. of *Bargadars* recorded till April 1985	Percentage increase
Midnapur	8,950	112,721	169,419	50.2	2,93,698	73.3
24 Parganas	2,794	84,138	117,239	39.3	1,64,986	40.7
W. Dinajpur	2,016	64,130	76,206	18.5	95,304	25.3
Bankura	2,537	49,702	67,206	35.2	97,929	45.7
Malda	1,539	49,657	54,314	9.3	74,505	37.1
Burwan	2,155	49,905	55,347	10.9	1,06,528	92.4
Hoogli	1,843	46,905	55,347	17.9	91,568	65.4
Cooch Bihar	696	40,699	49,769	22.3	72,670	45.9
Birbhum	2,120	38,595	50,409	30.6	95,304	89.0
Murshidabad	1,949	35,870	40,972	14.2	70,450	71.9
Jalpaiguri	408	35,902	41,013	14.2	55,267	34.7
Nadia	1,009	26,402	32,547	23.2	52,764	62.1
Howrah	643	24,835	26,647	7.2	37,917	42.2
Darjeeling	374	8,149	8,582	5.3	12,573	46.5
Total	29,033	6,67,610	8,45,017	26.5	13,21,463	56.4

Sources: 1. Government of West Bengal (1969).
2. D. Bandyopadhyay (1980).
3. Government of West Bengal (1985).

labourers in West Bengal, whose number multiplied over the years at an alarming rate. According to census estimates, agricultural labourers as percentage of agricultural workers increased from 18.47 in 1951 to 20.24 in 1961. In 1971, the percentage went up to 35. There was a drop in the percentage to 32.95 in 1981 largely due to the fact that the definition of a 'worker' changed in Indian census. Those who worked for 183 days or more than 6 months were included as 'worker'. This led to a gross underestimation of the number of agricultural labourers. Anyhow, the rise in the percentage of agricultural labourers in some districts was phenomenal. For example, between 1961 and 1971 the percentage of agricultural labourers increased in Burdwan from 25 to 56.4, in Hoogli from 23.3 to 53.2, in Birbhum from 32 to 50 and in Howrah from 31.1 to 57.4.[12] The rise in the percentage is particularly noticeable in agriculturally advanced areas. Policies towards this vast number of workers began to change since the late seventies with the emergence of the Left Front in power.

A number of steps were taken to improve the condition of the agricultural labourers. For example, a minimum wage was fixed for a standard eight hour working day, subject to revision with the increase in the cost of living. Public works programmes were taken up to increase employment opportunities during the lean periods. Dasgupta (1984) noted that by the end of 1981 more than 141 million man days of work were created. During the year of flood and drought these programmes played an important role in controlling the migration of labourers. Land redistribution programmes among the landless agricultural labourers were also undertaken. According to one estimate, the land redistribution programme benefitted about 14 lakh families of agricultural labourers till the early eighties.[13]

Some writers are however, extremely critical of the land redistribution programme of the Left Front Government. Mallick for example, noted,

At the end of 1978, 1,005,148 acres had been distributed under the Estate Acquisition Act and 117,428 under the Land Reforms Act. But by the end of 1984 only 1,049,220 acres and 184,049 had been vested indicating only 44,072 and 66,621 acres had been vested in the first six years of Left Front rule, a rate no better than under the previous Congress government. The Land Reforms Minister stated in the assembly that from the election of the Left Front till mid 1982 150,000 acres had been vested and 120,000 distributed,

[12] District Census Handbooks.
[13] Dasgupta (1984: A146).

which meant that 1 million acres had been vested before the Left Front came to power and 630,000 acres distributed already. The 799,224 distributed by the end of 1984 went to 1,572,531 persons or about 1/2 acre per beneficiary. (1993: 45)

Mallick's figures show that the Left Front achieved little compared to the earlier regime. However, Mallick fails to note that the redistribution figure is bound to be high in the pre-Left Front period as provisions of the new Act are easy to implement at the initial stage. The redistribution programme became tardy in course of time as the Left Front had to face an unsurmountable number of court cases relating to vesting of land and its redistribution. Mallick (1993) has done extensive statistical exercise in order to show negative effects of the agrarian reforms programme of the Left Front.[14] I have pointed out some shortcomings in his observations. In this context, it may be noted out that Mallick leaves out another possibility. The introduction of new technology might worsen land distribution. In the absence of appropriate state programme, the technological growth can only help the rich farmers. This kind of land consolidation has taken place in many parts of northern India in the late sixties and early seventies. Rudra (1982a) has dealt with this issue in his well-known study on the development of capitalist farming in agriculture in Punjab. The effects of land redistribution programme will be discussed later in this chapter. Before that, let us take a look at the growth of new technologies in West Bengal in the seventies and eighties.

3.2 THE NEW TECHNOLOGY IN AGRICULTURE

The first part of this section deals with two kinds of issues. First, it focuses on the nature of technological growth in West Bengal agriculture and second, it examines the impact of technological growth on crop production. In the second part, an attempt has been made to analyse the role of the state intervention in bringing about a technological change. All these developments in West Bengal agriculture have significant implications as far as the structuring of agrarian class relation is concerned. The impact of agrarian class relation on agricultural productivity too merits a close examination.

New technologies in West Bengal agriculture became popular from the late sixties with the irrigation extension programme, both surface and underground, and with the popularity of HYVs, fertilizers and

---

[14] Mallick (1993).

pesticides. In some areas, the Intensive Rural Development Programmes (IRDP) helped in distributing HYVs, fertilizers, pesticides as well as irrigation at a subsidised rate. According to the 1971-2 NSS report, fertilizer was used for about 58 per cent of West Bengal's irrigated land during the late sixties. Farmyard manure was used for about 65 per cent of irrigated land. Prior to this period, the use of chemical fertilizer was quite low, only 8.3 kg nutrient per hectare of grossed cropped area. In 1978-9, the use of fertilizer went up to 37.3 kg nutrient per hectare of land, an all time high.[15]

Data on the use of HYVs are not available in official reports. However, Boyce (1987) calculated HYV intensities from unpublished data of the Directorate of Agriculture of the Government of West Bengal and noted that in the 1978-9 period, HYV intensity or percentage area under HYV in the case of *aman* was 24.0 and for *aus* 34.4. Boyce added a note of caution as he observed that the figure was a bit inflated for over-estimation bias. Whatever may be the over-estimation bias, the success of HYV *boro* cultivation in West Bengal since the early seventies is a well known fact. Many writers have pointed out the growing popularity of the 'miracle seeds'.[16] The growth of irrigation helped the spread of both HYV seeds and fertilizers in rural West Bengal.

However, the use of irrigation, HYVs, fertilizers was not uniform in all the districts. Variations in the use of different types of irrigation facilities are worth noting. Districts like Burdwan, Hoogli, Howrah, Bankura, Midnapur and Nadia showed a marked improvement in the use of irrigation between 1971-2 and 1980-1 period (Table 3.3) Surface-water irrigation programmes helped districts like Burdwan, Birbhum and Hoogli, whereas underground water irrigated the rest. During the late seventies, two major government canals, Kangshabati and Damodar, together irrigated approximately 20 million or 80,000 hectares. The Teesta irrigation project improved the overall conditions in the late eighties. According to the Department of Agriculture report, in Nadia private and public STWs irrigated 37.6 per cent and DTW 41.9 per cent of net cropped land. Inter-district variations in the use of HYVs and fertilizers are also noticeable. Lack of data on HYV intensity over a period of time does not allow us to compare the position of various districts with regard to the use of HYVs. However, the data provided by the Department of Agriculture of the Government of West Bengal on HYV

[15] Boyce (1987).
[16] Bandyopadhyay (1975), Frankel (1971).

intensity for 1978-9 period shows that, in the case of *aman* paddy, Burdwan, Hoogli, Darjeeling and Nadia accounted for between 35 and 46 per cent of gross cropped area under HYVs. In the case of *aus* paddy, districts like Burdwan, Birbhum, 24 Parganas, Howrah and Purulia had covered cent per cent of their land under HYVs. Once again the performance of the Nadia district with regard to the use of HYV seeds is better than many other districts in West Bengal. Fertilizer intensity or nutrient kg per hectare per crop increased in Hoogli from 42.9 in 1970-2 to 101.5 in 1978-80. During the same period, it went up from 21.2 to 59.6 in Burdwan, 23.9 to 176.8 in Howrah and 11.9 to 49.3 in Nadia. According to Boyce, irrigation intensity (gross irrigated area ÷ net irrigated area) in Nadia was 1.54 whereas in the state as a whole it was 1.28. Only Hoogli district surpassed Nadia's record of irrigation intensity where it went up to 1.69 (1987: 173). Crop-wise comparisons of fertilizer use at the state level show that fertilizers are used more intensively in the post-*kharif* seasons and mostly for the commercial crops. The districts-level data show the complementarity of three major agricultural inputs, namely, irrigation, HYVs and fertilizers. Both HYV and fertilizer intensities are

TABLE 3.3: PERCENTAGE OF GROSS CROPPED AREA IRRIGATED IN WEST BENGAL DISTRICTS BETWEEN 1971-2 AND 1980-1

Districts	1971-2	1980-1
Burdwan	66.7	81.3
Hoogli	45.9	62.1
Birbhum	63.4	58.1
24 Parganas	8.5	21.5
Nadia	10.8	23.4
Murshidabad	20.4	52.0
Bankura	45.9	40.8
Midnapur	16.7	28.6
Howrah	24.4	42.1
Jalpaiguri	6.3	7.7
Darjeeling	38.9	57.5
Malda	13.1	21.2
West Dinajpur	5.1	18.0
Cooch Bihar	2.3	11.1
Purulia	26.7	17.1
West Bengal	24.3	45.5

SOURCE: Government of West Bengal, Directorate of Agriculture Annual Report, 1983.

high in the districts where the percentage of irrigated gross cropped area is high. For instance, in Burdwan irrigation intensity is high, correspondingly high are its HYV and fertilizer intensity. This is also true of districts like 24 Parganas, Hoogli, Nadia and Murshidabad.[17]

The spread of new technologies did not influence the process of mechanization like the use of tractors, threshing machines and crop cutting machines as they did in other parts of India. These machines were found unsuitable for two reasons. Firstly, these machines were of very little use in extremely fragmented agricultural plots. Transfers of land on a large scale and inheritance laws led to land fragmentation in West Bengal and tiny plots became unsuitable for large machines. Secondly, the use of machinaries was also unpopular on the ground that, in a labour-surplus rural economy, their use could create labour displacement. The state policies did not favour the spread of labour displacing machines in rural West Bengal.

In the eighties, there was a further increase in the use of new technologies in agriculture. The total irrigated area which was 51.35 thousand hectares in 1985-6 increased to 84.50 thousand hectares in 1988-9.[18] During this period, the expansion of underground irrigation facilities under minor irrigation programmes was particularly significant. The performance in surface water irrigation programmes was equally noteworthy (Table 3.4). The Teesta Barrage project, a well known project of the Left Front Government was launched for the expansion of irrigation

TABLE 3.4: EXPANSION OF MINOR IRRIGATION PROGRAMME (ADDITIONAL) BETWEEN 1985-6 AND 1988-9 (*in thousand ba*)

Year	Area under underground water	Area under Surface water	Total
1985-6	45.00	6.35	51.35
1986-7	37.65	16.05	53.70
1987-8	46.65	15.96	62.61
1988-9	49.50	35.00	84.50

SOURCE: *Economic Review, 1988-9*, Government of West Bengal.

[17] Boyce (1987) examines in detail the nature of complementarity of major inputs in West Bengal agriculture. See also Boyce (1986) and Shah (1993).

[18] Economic Review, Government of West Bengal, 1989-90.

TABLE 3.5: USE OF FERTILIZER IN WEST BENGAL
BETWEEN 1986-7 AND 1988-9 (*in metric tonnes*)

Type of Fertilizer	1986-7	1987-8	1988-9
Nitrogen	3,04,023	3,47,653	4,02,507
Phosphorus	1,13,827	1,28,916	1,59,717
Potassium	81,371	84,661	1,09,614

SOURCE: *Economic Review, 1988-9*, Government of West Bengal.

in North Bengal. In 1986-7 and during the *kharif* season, the project succeeded in providing water to 2000 hectares of land. In 1987, the irrigated area under the Teesta Project increased to a total of 7000 hectares of land.

Throughout the eighties, the state government made more efforts to popularize the use of HYV seeds and fertilizers. In 1986-7, 12.71 lakhs of mini kits were distributed among small and marginal farmers.[19] The number increased to 18.39 lakhs in 1987-8. An upward trend in the use of various kinds of fertilizers, e.g. nitrogen, phosphorus, and potassium, could be noticed particularly for *aman* and *boro* paddy and wheat (Table 3.5). Besides this, the disbursement of loans for agricultural purposes by the commercial and cooperative banks reached an all-time high in the late eighties. The commercial banks offered 80.80 crores and cooperative banks 59.55 crores rupees of loans to small and marginal farmers for agricultural production.

The popularity of irrigation and other agricultural inputs had an obvious effect on both the yield rate and cropping intensity in West Bengal in the sixties and seventies. The Bureau of Applied Economics and Statistics (BAES) data on food production showed a rise in wheat production from 71,000 tonnes in 1967 to a peak of 527,000 tonnes in 1976. The data of the Department of Agriculture (DA) of the Government of West Bengal showed a much sharper rise of about 1,187,000 tonnes in 1975. This kind of rise in wheat production could not have been possible without an intensive use of the HYVs and fertilizers. The BAES data on productivity of *boro* rice (the winter crop) reveals a similar pattern. The BAES data showed a rise from 40,000 tonnes in 1966 to 1,264,000 in 1978.[20] However, the productivity of the *aman* crop was not as

[19] Between 1977-8 and 1982-3, 46 lakhs free minikits were distributed. Each mini kit included HYV seeds, fertilizers and pesticides.

TABLE 3.6: PRODUCTIVITY OF *AMAN, BORO,* AND WHEAT IN
WEST BENGAL BETWEEN 1960 AND 1975 (*in thousand metric tonnes*)

Year	Aman	Boro	Wheat
1960	4899.5	37.7	25.7
1961	4368.8	32.8	34.4
1962	3973.0	26.8	30.6
1963	4810.3	29.0	32.7
1964	5131.1	27.1	27.9
1965	4385.4	36.9	34.0
1966	4254.3	40.0	45.5
1967	4493.7	110.6	71.1
1968	4830.0	221.9	268.1
1969	5089.7	316.7	481.9
1970	4694.7	534.4	868.1
1971	4608.0	934.0	921.2
1972	4190.7	728.9	688.0
1973	4373.9	729.2	628.8
1974	4812.8	856.4	836.8
1975	5181.2	899.8	1187.2

SOURCE: Department of Agriculture, Government of West Bengal.

steady as that of wheat or *boro. Aman,* which accounted for over
half of West Bengal's gross cropped acreage, showed an output
growth rate below the all crop trend (Table 3.6).

In 1987-8, foodgrain production went up to 103.05 lakh tonnes from
96.11 lakh tonnes in 1986-7. The production of paddy increased from
84.63 lakh tonnes in 1986-7 to 92.71 lakh tonnes in 1987-8. There was
an increase in the yield of both *boro* and *aman.* Contribution of three
varieties of paddy and other crops to the overall production of foodgrains
between 1985-6 and 1987-8 are presented in Table 3.7. The data not
only show an increase in the yield rate of some of the major crops but
also point out an increase in the acreage of land under cultivation for
crops like *boro, aus,* paddy, oil seeds and potatoes.

Of all the crops, the spread of new technologies made a significant
impact on the *boro* crop cultivation. Most of the *boro* crop is now
cultivated with HYV seeds and under controlled irrigation.
Bandyopadhyay (1978) noted that a new form of entrepreneurship has
emerged in *boro* cultivation. Entrepreneurs lease the land from the large
land-owners holding land in dispersed fragments and those who lack

[20] Boyce (1987: 74).

TABLE 3.7: AREA, YIELD AND YIELD RATE OF MAJOR CROPS OF WEST BENGAL, 1985-6 TO 1987-8

Principal Crops	1985-6			1986-7			1987-8		
	Area (000 ha)	Yield Rate (kg ha)	Total Yield (000 tonnes)	Area (000 ha)	Yield Rate (kg ha)	Total Yield (000 tonnes)	Area (000 ha)	Yield Rate (kg ha)	Total Yield (000 tonnes)
Aus	483.1	1,119	540.6	637.4	1,114	710.1	616.2	1,064	655.3
Aman	4083.3	1,475	6023.0	4059.2	1,403	5694.1	4067.2	1,506	6127.2
Boro	512.3	2,786	1427.2	679.4	3,030	2058.8	792.2	3,142	2489.3
Total	5078.7	5,380	7991.0	5376.0	5,547	8463.0	5475.6	6713	9271.8
Wheat	305.1	2,421	738.7	397.7	1,717	682.6	374.2	1,801	673.9
Pulses	421.0	628	264.3	353.6	564	199.6	362.8	626	227.0
Non level	97.5	1,373	133.9	118.4	2,244	265.7	94.2	1,408	132.8
Total	5902.3	1,546	9127.9	6245.7	4525	9610.9	8312.0	3835	103.37
Jute	730.7	1,820	7389.8	517.5	1,723	4950.4	423.7	1,545	3637.6
Oil Seeds	371.0	630	233.6	423.3	623	263.6	590.1	857	505.8
Patatos	138.4	19,930	2757.6	173.1	20,469	3542.6	179.9	21,848	3787.0
Total	1240.1	22,380	10381	1113.9	22,815	8756.6	1193.7	23,450	7930.4

SOURCE: *Economic Review, 1988-9*, Government of West Bengal.

command over resources sufficient to cultivate a second paddy crop.[21] Bandyopadhyay (1978) found that, with an investment of Rs. 500 per *bigha*, an enterprising farmer can make a net profit of Rs. 600 within a period of three months. The rate of return is particularly high in the case of *boro* as all essential material inputs and water were provided at a subsidized rate by the state development agencies, e.g. West Bengal State Seeds Corporation, National Seeds Corporation, West Bengal Agro-industries Corporation. *Boro* cultivation became popular particularly in the districts like Burdwan, Hoogli, Nadia and Midnapur where water supply during the winter was ensured through tubewell irrigation programmes.

Technological growth and increase in food production in West Bengal in the seventies and eighties became possible because of the institutional support provided by the local level organizations, e.g. block development offices, banks and cooperatives. District rural development agencies were entrusted with the task of spreading technologies in rural areas. Whenever necessary, local level government institutions sought support from *panchayats* and peasant associations for implementing government programmes. The gigantic task of *barga* registration can be cited as an example. It needs to be stressed that the state does not have complete control over all the institutions. As a unit in a federal structure, the state in West Bengal has to share power with the Centre. This can create hurdles in the adoption and implementation of land reform programmes. The state confronted such hurdles at the time of amending the acts, as all amendments to land reforms acts have to be ratified by the Central Government.[22]

Besides support from the state and its various institutions, technological growth and rise in food production became possible for enterprising skills of small farmers, especially those owning less than 5 acres of land. As mentioned earlier, this group is now the most important land-owning category in the state. Agricultural improvement in the state would not have been possible without the skill of this category of peasantry. Later, in this chapter, the various aspects of production organization of small farmers in rural West Bengal and the factors which motivated them in using the new technologies have been discussed.

[21] Bandyopadhyay (1975: 700-1). See also Bandyopadhyay and Biswas (1978), Harriss (1993).

[22] In one case (Amendment Act, 1971), it took more than five years to get approval from the Centre.

A great deal of controversy exists on the question of productive efficiency under sharecropping arrangement. Economists in India, by and large, agree with the Marshallian approach on this question. Marshall's (1920) well-known theory that sharecropping implies an inefficient allocation of resources and less productive than land under owner cultivation finds support in the writings of Bardhan and Srinivasan (1971), Bell (1977) and others.[23] However, the critics of Marshallian approach, especially the Chicago School showed that sharecropping arrangements do not imply an inefficient allocation of resources. According to Cheung (1968) the chief protagonist of the Chicago school, the inefficiency argument is illusory, allocation under private property right is the same whether the land-owner cultivates the land himself, hires farmhands to do the tilling, leases the holdings on a fixed rent basis or shares the actual yields with his tenant.[24] In the context of sharecropping system in West Bengal, it is to be seen whether access to credit, other institutional support and tenurial security has led to more efficient use of the leased land. The problem has been discussed at length, with the help of field data, later in this chapter.

The shift in the emphasis in government plans to make small farming production arrangement as ideal type for agricultural growth can be noticed in the policy statements of the Left Front. According to the Draft Seventh Five Year Plan 1985-90 and Annual plan 1985-6:

There is remarkable evidence available from all the districts of the state, that the highest record of production, taking into account per acre yield of the crops and also the cropping intensity is obtained not from the land of the big or the middle farmers but from the poor farmers. What these poor farmers do not have by way of implements and other inputs, they over-compensate by fuller application of their labour. It follows therefore that if the ceiling surplus land is distributed to the poor farmers and they are assisted in terms of non-land inputs, then not only the inequality between the farmers gets lessened, but a definitive move is also initiated to increase the level of production.

This was a major departure from the established practice in the state of supporting better off farmers in order to raise agricultural productivity.

One of the far-reaching effects of such a shift in land policy was

---

[23] Empirical evidence provided by Rudra (1982a) goes against the Marshallian position.

[24] See Bagchi (1982) for a critique of both the models.

realignment of relations between different agrarian classes. Changes in the relations between the land-owners and *bargadars* on the one hand and land-owners and labourers on the other could be noticed in rural West Bengal in the seventies and eighties. Some recent studies, e.g. Davis (1983), Lieten (1982), van Schendel (1991) have shown the nature of these changes and their implications for West Bengal as a whole. Barring a few, most of the literature on changing land-ownership pattern in West Bengal show a new trend in recent years. Land reform policies of the government of West Bengal have altered the traditional land-power nexus.[25] The emergence of a new panchayati raj system, peasant associations in local level politics and government programmes like OB which aimed at strengthening the position of the weaker sections played an important role in eliminating land-power nexus. However, the problem that needs to be examined is that how far the changes in the land-holding structure or land-power nexus influenced the process of agricultural growth.

Experiments with land reforms in West Bengal and their short- and long-term consequences can be compared with experiments in Bangladesh. This has been done in the next chapter. On the surface, there are broad similarities in the programmes with land reforms in the two Bengals. A close scrutiny, however, will explore several inherent differences. Before probing this, let us take a look at the technological changes and land relations in Nadia and in one of its villages.

3.3 AGRARIAN CHANGE IN NADIA

In the last chapter, a brief survey on the agrarian condition in Nadia during the colonial period, especially in the early part of the present century showed how the district made progress in productivity and in expanding land acreage under cultivation and also in increasing cropping intensity. Agricultural growth took place in the district for a large number of factors. First, Nadia had an edge over other districts in terms of geographical location. It was a part of the active delta of the Ganges, much less burdened with the problem of lowness of level, soil salinity and excess water.[26] Its soil was composed of finer alluvial elastics. Further, it was situated close to the Tropic of Cancer making its temperature

[25] Many anthropological studies on local-level power structure, e.g. Danda (1971), Nicholas (1962) have shown the dominance of land-owning caste in rural politics in West Bengal.

[26] Pringle and Kemm (1928).

favourable for the cultivation of sugarcane and different kinds of vegetables. Thus, favourable climatic conditions and fertile soil helped agricultural growth in Nadia. Second, the development of communication network through roads and rivers was also conducive to economic growth. Proximity of the district to Calcutta city and access of agricultural produce to Calcutta markets helped the commercialization of agriculture. The huge whole-sale markets for agricultural produce in Calcutta attracted many land-owners to invest in agriculture. Besides this, the rate of growth of population since the beginning of the century was not large enough to marginalize the gains in the agricultural sector.

After 1947, a large number of official surveys were carried out in Nadia to study the nature of agricultural growth, the spread of new technologies, the productivity, landholding and tenancy structure, and so on. Surveys were conducted under the supervision of various central and state government agencies, e.g. NSS, BAES, DRDA, DA and Socio-Economic Evaluation Cell. Some of the data can be used here to show the nature of growth of new technologies in Nadia. The irrigation infrastructure developed rapidly in Nadia. The spectacular growth in irrigation took place in the district in the seventies and eighties. There was a marked improvement in the use of ground water irrigation in the late seventies. In 1970 the river lift pumps irrigated 4,500 acres, which increased to 22,400 acres in 1974-5. Similarly, in 1970-1 45,000 acres were brought under DTW, which increased to 51,000 in 1974-5. The increase in the acreage under STW was phenomenal, as it grew from 35,000 acres in 1970-1 to about 80,000 acres in 1974-5. The percentage of gross cropped area under irrigation increased from 10.8 in 1971-2 to 23.4 in 1980-1. As a result of ground water extension programme, significant growth took place in the yield rate of *aus, aman, boro,* wheat and jute in the mid-seventies. The rate of increase of irrigation for some

TABLE 3.8: CROP AREA IRRIGATED IN NADIA
BETWEEN 1970-1 AND 1974-5

Crop	1970-1 (in acres)	1974-5 (in acres)	Percentage increase
Jute	12,500	29,500	36
Aus	13,500	34,781	57
Aman	18,000	40,643	25
Wheat	55,800	1,31,897	36

SOURCE: DRDA Report, Nadia (1976).

of the major crops in the district between 1970-1 and 1974-5 can be seen in Table 3.8.

The expansion of underground water irrigation programmes played the pivotal role in agricultural growth. Of the various kinds of irrigation systems that were available underground water proved to be most useful in terms of timeliness, adequacy and reliability.[27] Moreover, the idea to expand the underground water irrigation was to be welcomed in an area where high potential to tap irrigation water existed but the level of utilization was extremely low.

The development of irrigation programme in Nadia helped in increasing the cropping intensity. Double and even triple cropping became widespread. Between 1970 and 1975, a phenomenal increase in the acreage under wheat was also noticeable. It became a popular second crop. An increase in the acreage under *boro* and jute also took place in some areas. Both were cultivated as a second crop. Second crop cultivation became popular in the district from the mid-seventies. HYV seeds, fertilizers were used for most of the second crop. Almost all the district-level surveys showed an increase in the use of HYVs, fertilizers and pesticides in Nadia in the seventies and eighties. Along with the technological growth, the food production data also showed a rise. The production of almost all major crops showed an upward trend. For instance, in 1960-1 the total production of rice was 217.8 thousand tonnes (TN) which increased to 238.1 TN in 1980-1. Wheat production increased from 2.6 TN in 1960-1 to 97.2 TN in 1978-9.[28] Upward trend was noticed also with regard to the production of other cereals and pulses. Between 1982-3 and 1987-8 period the production of foodgrains rose further, from 112.16 TMT to 203.69 TMT.[29] During the period, the rate of growth of foodgrains in Nadia district surpassed the state average. Significant increase in the area under rice cultivation and increase in food production in the eighties became possible due to the introduction of HYVs and other improved methods of cultivation. The phenomenal rise in wheat production in the district explains why there was a fall in the production of other cereals. The nature of agricultural growth in the district could be evident from the following figures. In 1960-1, the area covered under

[27] In a recent study, Shah (1993) pointed out that in comparison to tanks, canals, wells DTWs and STWs offer better quality irrigation service and also generate large irrigation surplus.

[28] Economic Review, Government of West Bengal, 1980-1.

[29] Ibid., 1989-90.

total foodgrains was 380.3 thousand hectares or TH, which increased to 401.6 TH in 1987-8, and production increased from 311.0 thousand tonnes or TT to 655.4 TT. What were the factors which made this kind of agricultural growth in Nadia possible? What was the role of the state in introducing improved methods of production techniques and providing assistance to the farmers? How far land reforms programme of the state helped agricultural improvement in Nadia? These are some of the issues which have been explored in this study.

The data on area under cultivation, production of some important crops like rice, wheat and other cereals in the district during the sixties, seventies and late eighties show clearly an alround improvement in the agricultural sector (Table 3.9). Moreover, in the eighties, Nadia became one of the intensively irrigated districts in the state. The rise in the use of DTW, STW and RLP helped the spread of irrigation at a faster rate. Till 1988, the state government distributed as many as 532 DTWs, 600 STWs and 319 RLPs. Besides, many private STWs and RLPs were also in use. Thus, the district became one of the chief beneficiaries of the state-assisted irrigation development programme. The irrigation facilities on such a scale made double and triple cropping possible within a short period of time.

However, the data on area under cultivation, production of crops and improvement in irrigation will not provide an overall picture of agricultural growth in the district unless other indicators of growth, e.g. improvement in socio-economic conditions of poor farmers, protection of rights of sharecroppers, increase in wages of agricultural landless labourers and emlpoyment opportunities are taken into account. This has been done in the following sections. It will have to be pointed out that the agricultural sector is linked with other sectors like education and health. An overall

TABLE 3.9: AREA (*in thousand hectares*), PRODUCTION (*in thousand tonnes*) AND YIELD (*in kg per hectare*) OF RICE, WHEAT AND OTHER CEREALS IN NADIA BETWEEN 1960-1 AND 1987-8

Year	Rice			Wheat			Other Cereals		
	Area	Prod.	Yield	Area	Prod.	Yield	Area	Prod.	Yield
1960-1	220.3	217.8	989	4.1	2.6	634	4.4	2.8	636
1970-1	209.5	223.2	1065	44.4	122.8	2766	4.6	3.4	739
1980-1	208.4	280.7	1347	44.0	72.1	1639	2.7	2.2	815
1987-8	271.3	493.2	1818	50.0	106.2	2124	2.1	1.5	714

SOURCE: Directorate of Agriculture Report, Government of West Bengal.

picture of growth and social justice can be obtained by studying other related sectors. However, this study deals with the problem of growth and equity in the agricultural sector only.

Like other parts of West Bengal, the number of large holdings began to decline in Nadia in the sixties. In 1971, 77.82 per cent of the holdings in the district were below 5 acres. They represented 43.75 per cent of the area under cultivation. A comparison of the data with 1951 agricultural census figures would show how a sharp drop in the percentage of holdings below 10 and 25 acres had taken place in Nadia (Table 3.10). No official figure is available on the further decline in the size of holding under 5 acres. However, block-level data clearly shows a trend towards disaggregation and emergence of small farmers as an important category in the district agriculture (Table 3.10).

TABLE 3.10: PERCENTAGE DISTRIBUTION OF NUMBER OF HOLDINGS (H) AND AREA UNDER SIZE CLASS (A) IN NADIA, 1951 AND 1971

| Size Class | 1951 | | 1971 | |
(in acres)	H	A	H	A
0-5	63.33	29.87	77.82	43.75
5.01-10.00	24.92	31.59	16.51	33.20
10.01-25.00	10.19	25.32	5.60	22.13
25.01 and above	1.56	13.22	0.07	0.92
Total	100.00	100.00	100.00	100.00

SOURCES: Census (1951).
Socio-Economic Evaluation Branch Report (1975).

However, agricultural growth has not been uniform in all the blocks in Nadia. The development of irrigation, the use of HYVs, fertilizers and also food production under Krishnanagar sub-division, especially in Karimpur, Tehotta and Nakasipara, made significant progress.[30] Under Ranaghat sub-division, both Ranaghat I and Ranaghat II blocks performed better than others. It is worth noting the nature of growth of new technologies in Ranaghat II since village Bira comes under its jurisdiction.

Ranaghat Block II had a geographical area of 273.66 sq km with 223 villages and 118 *mouzas*. In 1981, the block had a population of 211,134, of which 40.2 per cent belonged to the scheduled caste category. Most of them migrated to Nadia from various parts of East Bengal since the

[30] Khasnobis and Chakraborty (1989: 34).

time of Partition. During the late eighties, the net area under cultivation in the block was 41200 acres and double cropping was practised in 15201 acres. In 1988, there were 38 DTWs which irrigated 1549 hectares, and 72 public and 2648 privately owned STWs in the block which irrigated 144 and 7977 hectares, respectively.[31]

The Comprehensive Area Development Corporation (CADC) a project of the government of West Bengal for agricultural growth played a catalytic role in spreading new technologies in Nadia as well as in Ranaghat Block II.[32] In all, there are 20 CADC projects in the state which cover an area of 20,000 acres of cultivated land. The CADC activities aimed at providing irrigation facilities and distributing agricultural inputs like HYV seeds, fertilizers and arranging credit, storage and marketing facilities. The 20 projects of the CADC covered all the major agro-climatic zones of the state, e.g. Himalayan foot hills, laterite west, gangetic plain and saline southern part of the state.[33] Two CADC projects of Nadia district were located in Ranaghat Block II and Haringhata. The core programme of the CADC projects in Nadia was to set-up new ground water irrigation facilities through a network of DTWs and STWs and to facilitate the use of HYVs. Installation of CADC DTWs was carried out in full swing in the early eighties in Ranaghat II. The number of DTW increased from 3 in 1976-7 to 18 in 1980-1, and covered almost one-third of the block. In addition, the block had 186 STWs which served 30 per cent of cultivable land during the main crop seasons. We can get some idea about the season-wise command area utilization of CADC owned DTWs, STWs and River Lift Pumps (RLP) in Table 3.11. Command

[31] BDO Report, Ranaghat Block II.

[32] The growth in the number of DTWs and STWs in the state under the CADC programme is particularly impressive. Irrigated area under CADC DTW increased from 4,976 acres in 1976-7 to 18,874 acres in 1980-1. In the irrigated areas under CADC STW increased from 5585 acres in 1977-8 to 12,902 acres in 1980-1. Dasgupta (1982: 54).

[33] Many writers are critical of CADC programme. In a hard-hitting attack on the CADC activities, Bose (1976: 1951-3) argued that this was no solution to the problems of the rural poor. He stated that neither the programme is going to improve the overall productivity from land nor the condition of small farmers, sharecroppers and labourers. Even a Leftist politician like Konar (1976) was critical of the CADC programmes. Till 1976 CADC achieved very little in terms of raising yield rate and benefitting the rural poor. However, the data on the performance of the CADC since 1978-9 showed signs of improvement.

TABLE 3.11: SEASON-WISE COMMAND AREA UTILIZATION OF CADC
OWNED DTW, STW, RLI IN RANAGHAT II IN 1984-5 (*in acres*)

Type of Irrigation	Pre-*Kharif*	Season *Kharif*	*Rabi/Boro*
DTW	150	239	657
STW/RLI, etc.	34.6	332	1119

Source: Data Handbook, 1984-5, WB CADC, Calcutta, 1987.

area utilization was highest during the *rabi/boro* season. As a result, the
production of these crops showed marked improvement. The gains of
irrigation were particularly noticeable in the case of cultivation of post-
kharif crops. We can also take a look at the production and employment effects of the DTW in the CADC project area in Nadia district
(Table 3.12) The CADC installed DTWs not only helped in raising
productivity but also created additional man days for poor labourers.

However, the CADC's role in disbursing other inputs, e.g. fertilizers,
HYVs and pesticides, is not as impressive as water management. The
spread of HYV took place largely as a result of individual initiatives. In
Ranaghat II Block, out of a total of 4068 acres, 2517 acres (61.8%) were
used for HYVs *aman* and 1551 (38.2%) for other traditional varieties. For
aus and *boro*, HYVs and fertilizer use exceeded two-third area of the total.

In any case, CADC has provided a much needed push to the rural
economy with its extensive irrigation programmes. In the late eighties,
CADC's efforts to offer loans to the farmers for the purchase of inputs
helped to increase cropping intensity and yield rate in the block and
offered much needed assistance to newly registered sharecroppers under
the Operation Barga Programme. The spread of new technologies in

TABLE 3.12: PRODUCTION AND EMLPOYMENT EFFECT OF DTW
IN CADC PROJECT AREA OF NADIA DISTRICT

Crop	Per Acre Production (in qntl)	Additional Man days
HYV aman	4	40
Wheat	11	80
Potato	90	120
Boro	14	110
HYV aus	4	46

Source: CADC Report, 1974-8.

Nadia as well as in Ranaghat II block had made an impact on the land holding structure too. In the CADC project area of Ranaghat II block medium and big farmers owned as much as 48 per cent of the total land in the late seventies (Table 3.13). Two other categories of farmers, i.e. marginal farmers (owning between 1 and less than 1 acre) and small farmers (owing between 1 and 5 acres) had 50 per cent land in Ranaghat II project area. During the early phase of the CADC project, a tendency towards land consolidation was noticeable as the expansion of irrigated area and distribution of agricultural inputs encouraged landowners to consolidate as well as to invest large amount of money. However, measures to register *barga* lands and to offer tenurial rights to sharecroppers forced many big farmers who were also lessors of land to dispose off their landed property. As a result, during the early eighties, small and marginal farmers came into prominence in the land holding strucuture. The percentage of landless labourers was high in Ranaghat CADC project area in the late seventies as can be seen in Table 3.13. In 1981, the percentage of agricultural labourers went up to 46.9 in Nadia district. Some points may be noted about the growth of agricultural labourers in Nadia and Ranaghat. Of all the districts in West Bengal which experienced phenomenal growth in the number of agricultural labourers, Nadia occupies the fifth position (Table 3.13). Two factors are particularly relevant in explaining the growth in the number of agricultural labourers in Nadia during the last three decades. Firstly, Nadia, being a border district attracted a large number of Hindu migrants from Bangladesh. It is difficult to get an exact idea of the number of migrants in the district as no official figures are available to date. Problems of keeping track on the migrants have become complicated as they follow no clear migratory pattern. Though the largest influx took place at the time of the Partition in 1947 and during the Indo-Pak wars in 1965 and 1971, the Hindu migrants poured in even during the normal period.[34] This has reached such a point now that the Government of India is considering sealing of the border and issuing identity cards to the residents of the districts bordering Bangladesh. Anyhow, the migratory population swelled the number of labourers in the rural areas in Nadia during the last four decades. A large number of Namasudras, a scheduled-caste under the Indian Constitution, settled down in Nadia after migrating from districts like Jessore, Kushtia, Rajshahi and Dhaka.[35]

[34] Chakrabarti (1990).
[35] Bandyopadhyay (1990).

TABLE 3.13: LANDHOLDING BY DIFFERENT CATEGORIES OF
AGRICULTURAL FAMILIES IN RANAGHAT II CADC AREA, 1978-9

Type	No. of families	Percentage	Total land (in acres)	Percentage	Average land per Family
Landless	1605	36	—	—	—
Farmer	1418	31	2224	21	1.56
Small Farmer	886	20	3241	31	3.65
Medium					
Big Farmer	582	13	4963	48	8.52
Total	4491	100	10428	100	—

SOURCE: CADC Report, 1978-9.

Secondly, inter-district migration too led to the growth in the number of landless labourers.[36] As mentioned earlier, the development of industries in Kalyani and its proximity to Calcutta city made Nadia attractive to migrants. Those who were unable to find jobs in the industries tried their luck in agriculture as labourers or *bargadars*. Such inter-district migration is particularly noticeable from agriculturally backward districts like Malda and West Dinajpur to relatively advanced areas.[37] Natural growth of population, and a crude birth rate varying between three and four per cent per annum in the sixties and seventies caused further demographic pressure on the labour market in recent years.

The growth in the number of agricultural labourers and poor farmers offered a favourable condition for the peasant organizations to expand their activities. Nadia became an ideal breeding ground of peasant unions. The district unit of the Bengal Provincial Krishak Sabha (BPKS) of the CPI (M) and Khet Majdur Union of the CPI were active throughout the late seventies and early eighties in mobilizing labourers and peasants for the protection of tenurial rights, higher wages and better prices for agricultural products. The BPKS membership in Nadia, which was 15,033 in 1975-6, went up to 55,180 in 1977-8 and then on to nearly two lakhs in 1982-3 (see Appendices I and II). The rise in the membership may be considered

[36] Pakrashi (1971) presents a detailed account of the nature of migration immediately after Partition in 1947.

[37] See Chakrabarti (1990) for an account on migrants who arrived after 1965 and 1971.

TABLE 3.14: PERCENTAGE OF THE AGRICULTURAL LABOURERS IN
WEST BENGAL BETWEEN 1951 AND 1981

Districts	1951	1981	Percentage increase
Burdwan	25.0	56.4	125.6
Hoogli	23.3	53.2	128.3
Birbhum	32.0	50.0	56.2
24 Parganas	26.9	49.6	84.3
Nadia	20.9	46.9	124.4
Murshidabad	23.9	48.7	103.7
Bankura	23.8	45.4	90.7
Midnapur	16.5	36.3	120.0
Howrah	33.1	57.4	73.4
Jalpaiguri	NA	31.9	—
Darjeeling	NA	24.3	—
Malda	17.3	46.2	167.0
West Dinajpur	12.1	42.0	247.1
Cooch Bihar	NA	34.0	—
Purulia	NA	32.6	—

SOURCE: A. Mitra (1953) and Government of West Bengal (1982).

as an indication of the growing popularity of the peasant unions within
a short period of time. The success in registering the names of
sharecroppers at the time of Operation Barga or in raising the real wage
for the agricultural labourers are all results of the intense movement of
various peasant organizations in Nadia. The contribution of peasant
associations in identifying surplus land in the district and their
redistribution among the poor peasants is equally significant. By the
middle of 1985, about 15 thousand acres of land were distributed in
Nadia with the help of peasant associations.

Among various factors which helped the process of unionization in
Nadia, the role of the Namasudra caste solidarity deserves special
mention.[38] The Namasudras formed caste associations in Jessore, Khulna
and Kushtia as early as in the thirties to fight upper caste domination.
Bandyopadhyay (1990) noted two sides of Namasudra caste movements
in Bengal in the thirties and forties. On the one hand, their movements
encouraged a demand for higher ritual status and thereby threatened
the hierarchical structure of society; on the other hand, these movements

[38] Bandyopadhyay (1990).

provided an opportunity to express group solidarity.[39] At one point, the Namasudras distanced themselves from nationalist politics to air their grievances against the caste domination in the Congress party. Their caste association became an important political force in course of time. Even after Partition in 1947 and political changes on a wider scale, the Namasudras who migrated from Eastern Bengal and settled down in the bordering districts of West Bengal showed a sense of solidarity by re-establishing caste associations and maintaining close links with fellow caste members. In the sixties and seventies, social and economic mobility helped some Namasudras to move up in the social ladder largely due to the policies of protective discrimination. Moreover, some Namasudra migrants who arrived in West Bengal with some capital managed to purchase land. The emerging social and economic cleavages among the Namasudras offered an ideal ground to mobilize the under-privileged under various peasant associations. Changes in the caste-type organizations to secular class-type organizations began to emerge among the Namasudras in the seventies and eighties. Thus, caste became important in secular rather than ritual context.

One more political development shaped the events in the district in the late seventies and eighties. In accordance with its electoral pledge, the Left Front reactivated the local-level power structure or the *panchayats*. Elections were held to these local bodies in 1978 and subsequently in 1983, 1988 and 1993. A major portion of financial resources of the state were disbursed through *panchayats* for development work. From 1979 to 1981, 300 crores of rupees were routed through the *panchayats* by the government departments. By the end of 5-year term of the Left Front in June 1983, 600 crores had been distributed through the *panchayats*. The major projects assigned to the *gram panchayats* by the Relief and Welfare Department was the 'food for work' programme. In December 1980; this was replaced by the National Rural Employment Programme. The Rural Reconstruction Programmes of the Relief and Welfare Department and Rural Works Programmes of the Development and Planning Department, both financed by the Central Government, created 56.63 million man days of

[39] Bandyopadhyay (1990) analysed how the Namasudras developed a distinct social and political identity of their own. In order to improve socio-economic position in a caste-based soceity, the Namasudras began to depend on their caste associations. See also Bandyopadhyay and Dasgupta (1997).

employment in 1978-9 reaching 70 million in December 1979.[40] The *panchayats* were reactivised mainly for two reasons; firstly, to give greater share of power to the rural poor and secondly, to manage the development programme funded from above.[41] Some recent surveys have shown positive effects of these steps. Lieten (1992), for example, noted that the character of public space has changed, poor peasants and agricultural labourers, including scheduled castes and scheduled tribes, have come to the forefront of public arena.[42] Westergaard (1986) too found more representation of the rural poor in *panchayats*. In various development programmes, e.g. Food for Work and National Rural Employment Programme, *panchayats* were given more power and resources. The programme for the registration of *barga* land too was carried out with the help of the *panchayats*. In Nadia as well as in other districts, *panchayats* began to play a crucial role in developmental programmes.

The chief aim of the *panchayats* under the Left Front Government was to put an end to land-power nexus in rural West Bengal. However, West Bengal *panchayati* system has been criticized by some writers. According to Bandyopadhyay (1993), *panchayats* in different tiers got fairly bureaucratized as *panchayats* leaders felt their primary duty was to look after assigned schemes and projects. In many areas, *panchayats* have done very little in terms of disbursement of loans to poor farmers, reclamation of vested land, protection of the interests of the sharecroppers. Mallick (1992) criticized the *panchayats* in West Bengal on the ground that they failed to dissociate themselves from the rural elite. The ideological work and raising of consciousness had never been done by the party. Most of the points raised by Bandyopadhyay and Mallick can be examined with the help of empirical data. On the contrary, some recent surveys in West Bengal villages, e.g. Lieten (1992), Harriss (1993), have drawn our attention to the role of the *panchayats* in successfully implementing development programmes and in breaking land-power nexus. The effects of various institutional changes that were set in motion by the Left Front Government during the late seventies can be analysed in greater detail with the help of the village-level data.

[40] Mallick (1993: 143).

[41] See Webster (1990), Westergaard (1986).

[42] With regard to representation of lower castes on *panchayats*, Lieten (1992) observed that most of the members who were elected on CPI(M) ticket in a block in Birbhum district belonged to SC/ST categories.

3.4 A CASE STUDY

Some aspects of land holding structure of village Bira during the Thak and Cadestral surveys have been discussed earlier. Thak survey report of 1856 included information on the total land of the village, Hindu and Muslim population, occupation and agricultural implements used by the villagers and the like. One of the important achievements accomplished by the Thakbast survey was to prepare a hand-drawn map of the *mouza*, showing locations of residential areas, tanks, rivers and crop plots. Right from the Thak survey the boundary of Bira *mouza* coincided with the village boundary. Villages in Bengal were surveyed more systematically in the thirties, with the launching of the Cadestral Survey (CS) operations. The land holding structure of the village came under close scrutiny at the time of the CS in 1935. The survey covered wide range of issues, e.g. land owned by the zamindars and their intermediaries, the types of land, the rate of revenue paid and the names of the *raiyats* or the actual tillers of land as well as *bargadars*. At the time of CS too, a *mouza* map was prepared in which residential areas, agricultural plots, tanks, rivers, etc., were demarcated.

The CS records in West Bengal were revised after Independence in accordance with the WBEAA and the WBLRA. This survey came to be known as the Revenue Survey (RS). This was the last survey which presented an account of the *zamindari* land holding structure and intermediary rights on land, more specifically rights of the *pattandars, darpattandars, bargadars* and *raiyats*. It included information on the types of land, amount of revenue and cess paid to the government and the different types of crops grown. The RS reports showed that at the time of Independence, most of the *zamindars* of the village were absentee landlords. Out of 29 *zamindars*, 9 lived in Santipur, 2 in Hoogli and one each in Burdwan, Kaliganj, Matiari, Aranghata, Krishnanagar and Ranaghat. The rest were residing in the village. A comparison of CS and RS data showed an increase in the number of *zamindars* from 18 to 29 signifying changes in the land holding structure. However, transfers of *zamindari* land were substantial between the CS and the RS periods.

The RS report presented a great deal of data on the nature of use of the village land during the final phase of the *zamindari* rule (Table 3.15). At the time of the RS more land was used for double cropping. Earlier high land was used only for the cultivation of the *aus* rice. RS data indicated that high as well as that low land was used for *aus* and *aman* crops.

TABLE 3.15: NATURE OF LAND USE OF BIRA
DURING THE REVENUE SURVEY

Land use	Land in Acres	Percentage
Cultivated High Land	242.87	63
Cultivated Low Land	123.10	32
Homestead	11.82	3
Tank	3.38	1
Garden	.77	—
Others	2.11	1
Total	384.05	100

The RS reports do not give any information on the yield rate or on the extent of the use of irrigation and agricultural implements. Nor do they present any information on the population, households or occupations of the residents of Bira. Nevertheless, the reports are useful as the survey presents a great deal of information on the land holding structure at the time of transition from British colonial rule to Independence.

No attempt has been made to survey the land holding structure of the village between 1960 and 1985. No survey could be found about the agricultural conditions in Bira during this period. Only the CADC collected information about the use of irrigation water in the village from time to time. The DRDA sent its survey team to the village a few times to collect information about crop production, cropping patterns and the use of HYVs, fertilizers during the mid-eighties. After a gap of about thirty years, the Government of West Bengal carried out a state-wide survey on the land ownership, cropping pattern, etc., in 1985. This was known as Land Reforms Survey (LRS). However, by the time we surveyed Bira in 1988, the LRS Report on the land holding structure was not ready for consultation.[43]

In 1988, at the time of fieldwork, the village had 132 households of which 109 belonged to the Hindus and 23 to the Muslims. The total population of the village was 808 (Table 3.16). The village had three residential areas, namely, (a) Hindupara, located on the northern part of the village with 70 Hindu migrant households (population 482); (b) Musalmanpara, one of the oldest residential areas in the village

---

[43] The Report would have given an idea about the changes in land-ownership, extent of *barga* cultivation and the nature of cropping pattern.

located on the south-western part with 23 households (population 138) and (c) Mathpara, situated on the north-eastern part of the village and comprised of 35 Hindu migrant households scattered over a large area (population 188). This residential area came up recently in order to accommodate a large number of Hindu refugees who arrived in Bira from neighbouring East Bengal districts since the 1965 Indo-Pak war. The cropping plots are located on the western and eastern parts of the village (see Map 9). It may be mentioned that Bira is surrounded by a few densely populated *mouzas*, e.g. Basta on the north, Sabdalpur on the east, Kanaipur on the south-western side, and Daula on the south-east. Some of the land-owners and *bargadars* of Bira were residing in these *mouzas*. Besides maintaining links with these neighbouring *mouzas*, Bira had close ties with the areas like Aranghata, a semi-urban locality situated 8 km away from the village where a whole-sale market, a railway station and a few block-level offices were located, and Ranaghat town located 20 km away from the village. Being a sub-division and an important trading centre, Ranaghat too attracted the residents of Bira as its railway station was well-connected with Calcutta as well as with Gede on the Indo-Bangladesh border. A branch line of the railways went to Bongaon from Ranaghat. Thus, the village had links with the trading centres by rail as well as by road. During the last one decade, communication facilities developed at a rapid rate in areas around the village.

Bira had a high percentage of migrant households right from the Partition in 1947. The number of migrant households went up to 93 in 1988, out of a total of 132 households (Table 3.16). The first major influx of refugee population took place from East Pakistan in 1947-8 following the Partition. A large number of Hindus belonging to Namasudra caste

TABLE 3.16: POPULATION, HOUSEHOLDS AND NUMBER OF MIGRANT HOUSEHOLDS IN THREE RESIDENTIAL AREAS OF BIRA, 1988

Residential Area	Households	Percentage	Population	Percentage
Hindupara	74	56	482	60
Musalmanpara	23	17	138	17
Mathpara	35	27	188	23
Total	132	100	808	100

NOTE: Migrant households from East Bengal include both migrants from the then East Pakistan and Bangladesh.

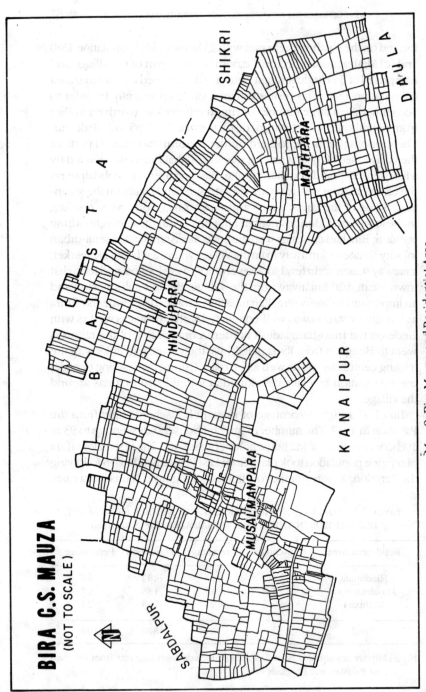

Map 9. Bira Mauza and Residential Area.

arrived from the neighbouring districts of Jessore, Khulna, Kushtia and Pabna. The arrival of the Namasudras in Bira led to some changes in the settlement pattern. The Muslims left the northern part of the village and moved to the old residential area in the south-east. The newly occupied area of the Namasudras became known as Hindupara. Most of the residents of Hindupara arrived between 1947 and 1964. Those who migrated at the time of 1965 Indo-Pak war or during the 1971 war of liberation for an independent state of Bangladesh had settled down in the new residential area called Mathpara. The immigration to Bira is a never-ending process. Immigrants are still pouring in. A number of families came to settle down in Mathpara in the eighties. Year-wise break down of the inflow of migrant population would show the trend in migration. During the first 10 years after Partition, from 1947 to 1957, 42 households arrived in the village. This was the peak period in migration. During the second phase, from 1958 to 1967, only 10 households made their way into the village and settled down in Mathpara. Most of the migrants arrived at the time of Indo-Pak war in 1965. During the third phase, between 1968 and 1977, 32 migrant households arrived in the village. Most of these households left fearing annihilation when the war of liberation broke out in 1971. Migratory movement since then has been slow. Between 1977 and 1988 only 9 households arrived from the neighbouring districts of Kushtia. In fact, most of them are short distance migrants who came from Kushtia-Nadia border areas.

The migratory movement had one other distinct characteristic. It was a caste- and community-based movement. Most of the migrants of the village belonged to the Namasudra caste. Sometimes three/four Namasudra families arrived in a group and settled down in the same village. Initially, these families shared a common house and a kitchen. A common guru, common religious festivals and customs helped the Namasudras to maintain social solidarity which they looked for after being uprooted. A cohesive, community-based social organization helped them to tide over the initial crisis of settling down in the new area.[44]

Migration which took place immediately after Partition in 1947 or after the Indo-Pak war in 1965 and 1971 was largely a result of communal tension or military atrocities. However, migration during the normal periods, e.g. in the late sixties or in the late seventies and eighties, took place due to the commonly known *push* and *pull* factors. Economic opportunities in West Bengal, better prices for agricultural goods and

[44] Bandyopadhyay (1990), Bandyopadhyay and Dasgupta (1997).

better wages for agricultural labourers pulled the migrants towards West Bengal during the normal period. A growing pressure of population on land, acute landlessness and political instabilities acted as the *push* factors on the other side of the border. In the absence of strict surveillance at the border, the number of migrants had multiplied over the years.[45] Besides migration from the other side of the border, internal migration, mostly from village to village or from town to village was also common. The number of such migrant households is small as compared to migrants from Bangladesh. Only three households in Musalmanpara and two in Mathpara reported this kind of movement from neighbouring villages to Bira.

Migration process has influenced land-man ratio in a significant way (Table 3.17). The percentage increase of population since the sixties has been particularly high. The 1981 census reported a high increase of 19.2 per cent mainly due to the war in 1971. Two obvious outcomes of this kind of increase in population and changes in land-man ratio are land fragmentation, small farming arrangements and swelling in the number of landless workers.

The process of migration has influenced not only the demographic composition of the village but also its economy and politics. The Namasudra refugees who were well known as enterprising farmers in East Bengal had brought with them the immense knowledge of cultivation

TABLE 3.17: POPULATION AND LAND-MAN RATIO IN BIRA

Year	Population	Percentage Increase	Land per Man (in acres)
1852 [a]	74	—	.51
1951 [b]	521	604	0.07
1961 [b]	575	10.3	0.6
1971 [b]	612	6.4	0.16
1981 [b]	730	19.2	0.5
1988		10.6	0.4

SOURCES: [a] Thak Survey.
          [b] Census Reports.

[45] The problem has reached a new height in recent time and forced the Government of India to identify and deport Bangladeshis. Unchecked migration has given rise to illegal trades in the bordering districts of West Bengal and Bangladesh. For an account on the smuggling in the border areas see van Schendel (1993).

of various crops. They were instrumental in introducing new crop cultivation and new techniques of production in the village. Within a short time, the Namasudras made their mark as skilled farmers in Nadia as well as in other bordering districts. Being refugees, the Namasudra cultivators realized the importance of hard labour and enterprising skills in a new land. In course of time, they began to play an equally important role in the block and village-level politics. As explained earlier, on many occasions, caste solidarity helped political mobilization and political support.

The Muslim population in Bira has remained stationary during the last three-four decades. Only one Muslim family had left for East Pakistan at the time of Partition. Besides this, individual members of some of the Muslim families had left in the early fifties but subsequently returned to Bira. They stayed back at the time of Partition in 1947 and during the periods of war in 1965 and 1971 for several reasons. First, the numerical dominance of the Muslims in many surrounding villages and blocks helped to dissipate communal tensions on these occasions. In 1947, the efforts of the Muslim leaders belonging to the Congress Party in Nadia to mobilize Muslim brethren against mass exodus to East Pakistan helped to check forced migration. Some Muslims were quick enough to realize the remote chances of further threat to their lives in newly independent secular India. The Muslims, like the Namasudras, too have played their part in the economic transition in the village. The use of irrigation, agricultural inputs like HYVs and fertilizers is popular among the better off Muslim land-owners and sharecroppers. Production organizations of some of the Muslim farmers of Bira have been discussed at length later in this chapter in order to show their skills and entrepreneurship. Their role in *panchayats* and peasant organizations too has been examined.

Technological growth in Bira, especially the growth of irrigation, HYVs, fertilizers and pesticides, began to take place from the late sixties. The irrigation infrastructure in the village had been developed by the CADC. It opened up a DTW on the north-eastern part of the village in 1965, which had a command area of 100 acres on an average. The main objective of the CADC irrigation programme was to ensure supply of adequate water in the high lands for *aus, boro,* and other winter crops. Within a short period after its inception, the DTW became indispensable for crops like *boro,* jute, *aus,* rapeseeds, mustard, potato, wheat, pulses, sugarcane, groundnut and other vegetables. The DTW was also used for *aman* crop whenever the monsoon got delayed. In 1987-8, the DTW was used for *boro, aus, aman,* mustard and vegetables. During this period, the DTW succeeded in supplying water in 40.03 acres of *aus*, 25.06 acres of rapeseed and 11.50 acres of mustard land. Compared to other crops, irrigated acreage under *aus* was below the average in this year as the supply of water from the DTW to land under *aus* crop was affected due to a technical fault in the pump. The acreage under *aman* only included high lands.

Besides the DTW, both privately owned and CADC-controlled STWs are in use in Bira. Some of the privately-owned STWs are hired out at the rate of Rs.10 per hour during the post-*kharif* season. Compared to STWs, the DTW water rate is cheaper. The farmers pay only Rs.240 a year for DTW water for an acre of *boro* land, considering the fact that water consumption in an acre of land is extremely high for *boro*. Water requirement for HYV transplanted *aus* is also high, and the DTW water rate for an acre of HYV *aus* is Rs. 125 for the high land and Rs. 60 for the medium level land. The DTW water rates (per acre) for potato is Rs. 100, for sugarcane Rs. 100 and for vegetables Rs. 100 for every six months. One pays nearly double of this amount for STW water.

Moreover, the DTW water users have the option of taking time in repaying water cess to the CADC. As a result, DTW water has become much sought after in the village. Both CADC DTWs and STWs fulfill the net demand for water during the *kharif* and post-*kharif* seasons. The water is particularly useful in the event of an inadequate rainfall.

Some writers are sceptical about the role of state-run tubewells in the spread of irrigation. Shah (1993) observed that state tubewells everywhere are afflicted by the problem of inefficiency, poor maintenance, long shut-down periods, erratic and insufficient power supplies, dominance of the powerful, right-of-way problems, arbitrary behaviour of the tubewell operator and strong propensity of the system towards corruption. Except erratic and insufficient power supplies, which is a general problem all over the state, state-run DTWs and STWs have performed reasonably well in the villages in supplying water during the dry seasons and in dealing with the problem of corruption and arbitrary behaviour of the pump operators. The village *panchayat* and peasant associations kept the necessary checks on the tubewell operators.

Three varieties of paddy are commonly grown in Bira, *aus*, *aman* and *boro*. *Aus* paddy cultivation is more popular than *aman* as the high land of Nadia is ideally suited for this crop. *Aus* is sown in the Bengali month of *Baisakh* (mid-April to mid-May) and harvested in *Bhadra* (mid-August to mid-September) whereas *aman* is sown in *Asadh* (mid-June to mid-July) and harvested in *Agrahan* (mid-November to mid-December). Irrigation water is more needed for *aus* than for *aman* as the monsoon season sets in only around June. The other variety of paddy, *boro*, which is sown in the Bengali months of *Paus* and *Magh* (around December-January) and harvested in *Baisakh* has flourished as a result of irrigation expansion programme. *Boro*, being a HYV crop, is entirely dependent on irrigation, fertilizers and pesticides for its growth. The deep and shallow tubewell irrigation has helped the farmers of Bira to bring more land under *boro* cultivation. The cultivation time of another important crop, jute coincides with that of *aus*. Therefore, farmers have an option to grow either *aus* or jute. Recent fluctuations in the wholesale price of jute have discouraged many farmers to cultivate this crop instead of *aus*.

The CADC controlled DTW is located in the high land area to ensure water supply at the time of *aus* and *boro* cultivation. The water from the DTW is available during the entire winter season. As a result, the farmers now grow a second crop in the high land, *boro* rice and vegetables like cauliflower, tomato, peas. Some enterprising farmers have produced even a third crop, mostly *aus* and two other kinds of vegetables during the rabi season. Therefore, the extension of irrigation network has made a positive effect on the cropping intensity.

The spread of irrigation has facilitated the use of HYV seeds in the village for crops like *aus, aman, boro*, jute and vegetables. The use of HYV *aman* and *aus* seeds, e.g. IR 050, increased the yield rate of *aman* by 10 *maunds* in a *bigha*. The CADC played an important role in selling HYVs at a subsidized rate. In 1987-8, the CADC fulfilled between 30 and 40 per cent demand for the HYVs in Bira. Besides CADC, the farmers depend on two other sources. HYVs are now available in the open market at a higher rate. This source is often tapped by the enterprising farmers when the CADC supply falls short. Secondly, the *aratdars* or wholesale traders for crops often supply HYV on the condition that the farmer will have to sell his produce to them at a cheaper rate after the harvest. Approximately 10 kg of HYV *aman* paddy seeds are required for a *bigha* of land, which in an open market would cost Rs. 15 and in CADC Rs. 10 only. The *aratdar's* price is higher than the CADC rate but slightly lower than the open market rate, and varies between Rs. 12 and Rs. 14. Multiple sources of HYVs helped its popularity in the villages. Fertilizer use is indispensable for HYV crops. In a *bigha* of HYV paddy land, a farmer spends on an average Rs. 250 on fertilizer which includes

40 kg of phosphate, 30 kg of urea and 12 kg of potash.[46] The CADC's role in supplying fertilizers is not as significant as HYVs. As a result, the farmers depend either on the open market or on the *aratdars* for regular supply of fertilizers. The deficit in the supply of fertilizers is often compensated by the farmers by using the traditional methods of fertilization. For example, the use of cowdung manure is still popular in Bira. Compared to chemical fertilizers, manures are cheaper and easily available to those farmers who own cows, bullocks and buffaloes. However, such manure fulfils only partial demand for fertilizers in the villages. Besides cowdung manure, the farmers often supplement their demand by using *dhaincha* (a local plant) in the field for fertilizing purposes. The practice is commonly known as green manuring. This plants takes about two months to grow. They are cut just before ploughing the land for *aman* paddy. The rotten leaves of the plant are mixed with the soil at the time of ploughing. The effect of this kind of fertilization lasts for about four years.

Pesticides too have become an integral part of cultivation in the village. The expenses on pesticide in a *bigha* of paddy land vary between Rs. 30 and Rs. 50. Although, about 200 gm of pesticide is required on an average in a *bigha*, the demand for pesticides fluctuates a great deal. In some years when pest attacks are acute, expenses on pesticides shoot up. Pesticides are needed more for *kharif* than for *rabi* crops. *Aus* paddy and some vegetables are prone to insect attacks. Anyhow, the use of major inputs like irrigation, HYVs, fertilizers and pesticides have become popular in recent times. The data on the use of these inputs also shows complementarity. A farmer who uses more water for cultivation is also found using a greater amount of HYVs and higher doses of fertilizers and pesticides to increase the yield rate. In fact, the development of irrigation has led to an extensive use of HYVs and fertilizers. Thus, one may consider irrigation as the 'leading input' in spreading new technologies in the village.[47] Irrigation has been successful in stabilizing fluctuations in production arising from variations in rainfall as well as in introducing a second crop. Most important of all, irrigation has made possible the use of other inputs for higher productivity.

[46] Urea requirement is less for *boro* paddy and is about 10 kg for a *bigha* of land.

[47] Ishikawa (1967) coined the term in the context of Asian agriculture. Many writers have shown the relevance of Ishikawa's thesis in Indian context. See Boyce (1987), Shah (1993).

The process of mechanization has been extremely slow in Bira. Tractors, threshing machines or power tillers are hardly used. Factors influencing the slow process of mechanization in the village are many. Firstly, from the point of view of land-owners, labour displacing machines are found unsuitable in the village as labour is cheap and easily available. The cost of machines would be higher than the expenses on labour. Secondly, small plot size would also discourage a farmer in using machines. The smaller size of holdings and fragmentation would stand in the way of maximum utilization of machines. However, lack of use of modern machines has not prevented the growth of other modern agricultural inputs in the village.

The yield rate of almost all major crops show an upward trend in recent years. For example, the yield rate of traditional variety of *aman* which was between 10 and 12 *maunds* per *bigha* increased to about 20 *maunds* a *bigha* in the land under HYVs. Such an increase could be noticed also in the case of other crops, e.g. *aus* paddy which increased from 8 *maunds* a *bigha* to 15 *maunds*. As far as cropping intensity is concerned, as pointed out earlier, the introduction of DTW in the high land areas has helped the farmers to grow a second crop and even a third crop during the rabi season. The increase in the gross cropped area (net sown area × cropping intensity) has led to an overall increase in the crop acreage. The rise in the aggregate output in the village is a result of both, an increase in the yield rate as well as an expansion in the gross cropped area.

Two kinds of problems merit attention in the context of technological growth in Bira. Firstly, which agrarian classes have gone for new technologies and improved productivity? And secondly, what are the effects of technological changes on the rural poor, especially on the landless labourers and sharecroppers?

In order to answer these questions, it will be necessary to point out the nature of agrarian class structure in Bira. A large number of writers have examined the problem of class structure in Bengal agriculture following classical Leninist and Maoist approach to divide rural society into landlords, rich peasants, middle peasants, poor peasants and rural proletariat.[48] The classification takes into account not only the extent of land ownership but also the relations of production. Mukherjee (1957),

---

[48] See, for example, Mukherjee (1957), Rahman (1986), Rudra (1982b). Beteille commented on the problem of this kind of classification, especially with regard to the overlapping categories (1974: 171-87).

for example, identified three distinct classes of peasantry in Bengal during the last phase of the British rule. At the top of the hierarchy, Mukherjee found the landed gentry, subinfeudatory landlords and prosperous non-cultivating or supervisory farmers. The self-sufficient peasantry occupied the middle rung, and other occupational groups like sharecroppers, agricultural labourers, service holders were at the bottom of the three-tier class structure. This kind of agrarian class structure has undergone considerable changes in recent times as a result of new land tenure policies. For example, the class of landed gentry, sub-infeudatory landlords has disappeared with the abolition of zamindari system. Secondly, the middle rung in the hierarchy now represents heterogeneous categories. This is also true of those who are at the bottom in Mukherjee's classification. For example, in some agriculturally advanced areas, leasing in of land by middle peasants is quite common. In such cases, lessees of land would occupy positions somewhat higher in the hierarchy. Similarly, leasing out of land by poor peasants can be noticed in some areas. Technological growth in rural West Bengal has created many such problems in conceptualizing agrarian hierarchy in clear terms.[49] More recently Patnaik (1987) classified West Bengal peasantry in terms of poor peasants, lower middle, upper middle and rich peasants, and landlords. According to Patnaik, on the basis of landholding, one can classify poor peasants as owning less than 1.60 acres, lower middle as owning between 1.61 and 4.60 acres, upper middle between 4.61 and 9.80 and rich peasants and landlords as over 9.81 acres. In an extremely fertile land where new technologies are in use a peasant household owning more than 5 acres would certainly belong to the class of rich farmers.

By taking into account primary occupations of the working members of the households and extent of ownership of land, a three-tier class structure can be drawn. Other factors like surplus production for the market, extent of land leased out, additional employment and income, the size of the household, the age and gender differences have been left out. Other things being equal, in the agrarian hierarchy in Bira, one would find those who belong to class I (rich farmers) own between 5 and 10 acres of land and carry on cultivation with the help of the wage labourers or sharecroppers. These land owners owned 42.24 acres of land (12 per cent) in the village in 1988. Most of them are surplus producing farmers. However, most land-owning households are in

---

[49] See Chapter IV for more discussions on the nature of agrarian hierachy.

TABLE 3.18: PRIMARY AGRICULTURAL OCCUPATIONS AND CLASS
POSITIONS OF THE VILLAGE HOUSEHOLDS

Primary Agricultural Occupations	Class position	Number of Households	Percentage
Land-Owner (over 5 acres)	I	6	5
Land-Owner (between one and five acres)	II	12	9
Land-owner-Sharecropper	III	61	46
Sharecropper	III	13	10
Landless Labourer	III	15	11
Labourer-Sharecropper	III	10	8
Labourer-Land-owner	III	9	7
Non-agricultural Occupations	—	6	4
Total	—	132	100

class II, owning between one and five acres of land. They are self-cultivating peasants, and hire labour only during the peak seasons. Some may lease out land. The land-owners owning less than one acre, sharecroppers, sharecroppers-cum-land-owners (with leased in and owned land not exceeding 2 acres), sharecroppers-cum-labourers and landless labourers occupy position in class III. Primary occupations and class position of 132 village households are shown in Table 3.18. The land-owner-cum-sharecroppers are numerically strong as they constitute 46 per cent of total households. In terms of size of holdings, those owning two acres or less than one acre control 37 per cent of cultivable land (Table 3.19). Therefore, undoubtedly this is not only the most numerous but also socially and economically the most important class. Those owning between one and five acres occupy 51 per cent of cultivable land. These sections played an important role in bringing about agricultural modernization in Bira.

A number of writers on 'green revolution' in Indian sub-continent are of the view that the technological growth can come about only with the active support of the rich peasantry. Byres (1972), for example, pointed out that only the rich peasants with larger personal resources and access to credit on reasonable terms were capable of taking advantage of such a technology. Small peasants and sharecroppers are thereby excluded because of lack of resources and acceptable collateral.[50] Rahman (1986)

[50] Byres (1972: 104).

too observed that in Bangladesh due to better access to capital and input markets, the rich farmers adopted the new technology more frequently than the smaller ones and the proportion of their land under HYVs was greater.[51] Rahman found some other trends like rich peasants resuming their leased out land, and/or becoming tenants at the expense of poor peasants and/or buying more land through distress sales. This brings us to the problem of size of holding and productivity. Bharadwaj (1974a) made significant contributions to the debate on the size and productivity in Indian agriculture. Sen (1964) first initiated discussions by pointing out that, by and large, productivity per acre would decrease with the increase in the size of holding. Sen's observations provoked an intense debate on the issue in the late sixties. Some economists expressed doubts on this kind of relations.[52] Bharadwaj drew attention to some of the crucial variables in the debate like differences in techniques as small holders may be using technically superior methods of production, enjoying qualitative differences in factor endowment in either land or labour or more intensive application of other inputs like labour, bullock power or irrigation. Apart from intensive land use cropping patterns also contribute to the relative higher value productivity on smaller farms. Bharadwaj's field data shows that the owner of small holding generally cultivate land more intensively and/or produce crops of greater value per acre. The market situation can affect the position of the small farmers considerably. This is why Bharadwaj argues that intensity in the cultivations and cropping pattern are in turn influnced by the particular characteristics of markets (for both inputs and outputs), by the resource position of the individual operator and by the nature and extent of his involvement in these markets.[53]

Bharadwaj's observations on the efficiency of tenants are worth noting too. She observed that those tenants who can secure land on the basis of a fixed rent system show greater interest to undertake irrigation for cultivation purposes. Lease arrangement has to be a secure one with the level of fixed rent remaining constant or changing predictably. On the other hand, if the tenant has a relatively weaker bargaining position or he is a tenant-at-will so that the landlord can deprive him of tenurial right, he will have very little incentive in undertaking investment in irrigation or in other such durable assets which are not shiftable.

[51] Rahman (1986: 29).
[52] Rao 1967; Rudra 1968.
[53] Bharadwaj 1974a; 1974b.

TABLE 3.19: SIZE OF HOLDINGS AND AMOUNT OF LAND
IN EACH SIZE GROUP, BIRA, 1988

Size of Holdings	Amount of Land	Percentage
0.00-0.50	60.95	17
0.51-1.00	72.53	20
1.01-1.50	58.53	16
1.51-2.00	36.12	10
2.01-2.50	18.17	5
2.51-3.00	24.29	7
3.01-3.50	22.32	6
3.51-4.00	3.89	1
4.01-4.50	12.69	4
4.51-5.00	4.81	2
5.00 and above	41.24	12
Total	355.54	100

This will work even better if the landlord parcels out his land in such small units that the tenant has to cultivate the small piece of land intensively to raise enough crop to secure his subsistence after paying the landlord's share.

Recent changes in the use of new technologies in Bira present an alternative scenario in which one finds an important role of a large number of small farmers and land-owner-cum-sharecroppers (Table 3.19). This was possible for two reasons. Firstly, various programmes for technological growth in agriculture aimed at offering incentives and institutional support to 'medium' and 'small farmers' so that they could adopt and utilize technologies to the fullest extent. Secondly, tenurial security to sharecroppers and strict enforcement of laws relating to tenancy improved the condition of small farmers-cum-sharecroppers. Both these points have been discussed in detail later in this section.

A sizeable number of land-owners of Bira are residing outside the village. In 1988, 56 per cent of village land was owned by those who were residing in the neighbouring villages or towns (Table 3.20) like Sabdalpur, Basta, Daula, Hossenpur, Kanaipur and Panchberia. Some were residing in places like Ranaghat, Aranghata and Calcutta. The absenteeism in land-ownership has led to two kinds of developments in the village. Firstly, absenteeism has given rise to sharecropping. In 1988, 55 per cent of the cultivable village land was under the control of the

TABLE 3.20: RESIDENCE OF THE LAND-OWNERS OF BIRA AND
AMOUNT OF LAND OWNED, 1988

Residence of the Landowners	Total Land Owned	Percentage (in acres)
Bira	155.69	44
Sabdalpur	64.48	18
Basta	33.22	9
Daula	10.47	3
Hossenpur	2.63	1
Kanipur	16.58	5
Panchberia	14.30	4
Aranghata	44.18	12
Ranaghat	1.44	—
24 Parganas	5.75	2
Calcutta	4.74	2
Total	353.48	100

sharecroppers who had to pay 50 per cent of the crop as rent to the owners of the land in the case of the main crop, e.g. *aman, aus, boro* paddy, and for such crops like jute, mustard seeds, rape seeds, peanuts, vegetables. Secondly, absenteeism had affected the spread of new technologies as the absentee land-owners were reluctant to invest on modern agricultural implements. However, changes are noticeable in recent years with regard to the use of new technologies and agricultural implements in the land owned by the absentee land-owners. The 'operation barga' programme which offered tenurial security to the *bargadars* in Bira encouraged the use of new technologies in the leased in land as the programme fixed the rent and offered material support. A large number of *bargadars* are now using modern inputs and irrigation. Various factors accounting for this kind of trend in the village are explained later in this section.

Production arrangements of land-owners who are residing in the village and owning more than five acres also show a tendency among them to invest more on new technologies. For instance, Kalipada Biswas, a 55-year-old Namasudra migrant-land-owner of 7.50 acres, uses both DTW and STW water to grow *aus, aman* and other cash crop like rape-seeds, peanuts and vegetables. He uses HYV seeds and fertilizers in the entire field. New technologies have helped Kalipada to increase cropping intensity as well as yield rate. HYV *aus* now helps Kalipada to get 15 *maunds* of crop in a bigha whereas traditional varieties used to give him a maximum 7 *maunds*. In 1988, an approximate cost of production of HYV *aus* in a *bigha* of land (including labour, seeds, fertilizers, pesticides, irrigation, etc.) was Rs. 770. The wholesale price of *aus* in the same year was Rs. 1250 for 15 *maunds*. This left room for earning profit from the cultivation of HYVs with the use of new technologies. Majammal Haq, a 62-year-old resident of Musalmanpara who owns 9.15 acres of land, too uses DTW and STW irrigation and HYVs and fertilizers. Like Kalipada he has gained as a result of rise in cropping intensity and yield rate. More such examples can be cited to show how new technologies are gaining popularity among the rich farmers in the village. Let us take a closer look at the production organization of small farmers and small farmers-cum- sharecroppers who could be considered as harbingers of technological changes in the village. This latter group deserves more attention as 60 per cent of agricultural households combine land-ownership with sharecropping.

Land-owners-cum-sharecroppers belong to an extremely mixed group in terms of the size of holding. Nearly one-third of them own between one and five acres but lease in land to improve their economic conditions. New technologies have become particularly popular among them. It needs to be emphasized that, in terms of control of the village land, the land-owners-cum-sharecroppers own and cultivate about 65 per cent of land, more than other group in the village. How is it that land-owners-cum-sharecroppers, who are not so receptive in other parts of green revolution areas, played such a major role in using new technologies in Bira? This is particularly worth investigating as most of the literature on the spread of new technologies in ushering in green revolution belittles the role of the small farmers and sharecroppers.[54] Writers are particularly sceptical about the role of the land-owners-cum-sharecroppers as differences in the use of modern inputs and yield rate are quite marked in the 'owned' and 'leased in' land. For example. Bell (1977) and Hossain (1977) who compared productivity in owned and tenanted land found cropping intensity, inputs use and yield rate were invariably better in owned land.[55] However, the development of new technologies has influenced land-owners in initiating dialogue with the sharecroppers and better terms and conditions on tenanted land have encouraged the later in raising yield by using new technologies.[56] Let us

[54] Byres (1972), Rahman (1986), Griffin (1974).

[55] See Rudra (1982b) for an excellent review of these literature.

[56] See Bhaumik (1993) for detailed discussion on this question.

take up the question of better terms and conditions for the lessees of land.

As mentioned earlier, the sharecroppers of Bira enjoyed tenurial rights as a result of a special programme called 'operation barga'(OB) launched by the Government of West Bengal. For the purpose of registering the names of the sharecroppers, the state government formed squads comprising the state-level officials, the District Land Reforms Officer, the BDO along with the members of the local units of the WBPKS. One such squad opened camps in Bira in 1977 recorded the names of the *bargadars* and distributed deeds on the spot. In 1979, when the OB came to an end, as many as 85 sharecroppers recorded their names in the village. The OB had been successful in recording the name of small as well as big *bargadars*. Between 1977 and 1979, the OB succeeded in registering the names of the *bargadars* cultivating a total of 124 acres. Some of these *bargadars* were residing outside Bira, in the neighbouring villages like Sabdalpur, Basta, Daula, Kanaipur and Panchberia. The residence of some sharecroppers outside Bira did not influence the efficiency and productivity as most of these neighbouring villages are located within a radius of about five kilometres and most of their land was located within the DTW/STW command area.

A special effort to disburse loans to sharecroppers and assignees of vested land was made right from the late seventies throughout West Bengal. For example during the *kharif* season in 1985, 5 lakh beneficiaries received loans from the commercial and *gramin* banks and cooperatives. Disbursement of loans at easy repayment terms helped the land-owners and sharecroppers to invest in HYVs, fertilizers and pesticides. During the 1987-8 period, 56 sharecroppers in Bira received DRDA loan from the bank amounting to Rs. 66,231,55.[57] The loan helped them to meet costs of new inputs.

A few cases may be cited to show the nature of enterprising skills among the small farmers and small farmer-cum-sharecroppers in the village. Gurupada Biswas, a 36-year-old small farmer-cum-sharecropper arrived in Bira as an immigrant from Jessore district in 1965 during the Indo-Pak War. Gurupada now owns 4 acres and leases in 1.7 acres from a land-owner residing in Aranghata. At the time of OB, Gurupada registered his name as a *bona fide* tenant. Most of his land is now located near the CADC DTW command area. He received a loan of Rs. 1600 after *barga* registration from the CADC to buy HYV seeds, fertilizers and other inputs. The use of modern inputs and irrigation helped him to raise

[57] DRDA Report, Nadia District, 1989.

the yield rate of most of the crop. The nature of profit from the cultivation of *boro* in Gurupada's case may be examined. The yield rate of *boro* varies between 20 and 15 *maunds* in a *bigha*. In 1988, the cost of production of *boro* in a *bigha* (including labour, seeds, fertilizers, pesticides, irrigation, etc.) was Rs. 825. In the same year, 20 *maunds* of *boro* fetched a price of Rs. 1625 in the open market. As a result, the profit from the cultivation of *boro* remained high. Such high returns are now encouraging farmers like Gurupada to invest more on new technologies in order to increase the yield rate as well as cropping intensity. With regard to the use of inputs in owned and leased in land, Gurupada makes no distinction at all. As a result of OB registration in the village, the land-owner gets only 50 per cent share of one crop (*aus* or *boro*), the entire earning from the seconds crop goes to Gurupada. This acts as an incentive now to invest more on leased in land. The sharecroppers of Bira now do not entertain the claim of the land-owners of their share on the second crop as they offer them more than 25 per cent of the produce of one crop, which is the officially recognized share of a land-owner who does not provide inputs. Similarly, Badal Biswas, a 37-year-old small farmer-cum-sharecropper who migrated from Jessore in 1956, belongs to the same genre of enterprising farmers. He owns 1.25 acres and leases in 2.66. His land-owner too is a resident of Aranghata. Badal registered his name at the time of OB and was able to receive a CADC loan of Rs. 3000. Like Gurupada, with the use of irrigation, HYVs, fertilizers and pesticides, Badal too managed to increase the cropping intensity as well as the yield rate. In this case too, the lessee pays only 50 per cent *aus* crop to the lessors and no other share of seconds crop. The rationale behind paying only 50 per cent of one crop to the owner of the land is the same as in the earlier case. In both these cases, the security of tenurial rights, access to agricultural credit and irrigation at a cheaper rate from the CADC helped to raise the economic conditions of land-owners-cum-sharecroppers. The OB thus provided much needed incentive to small farmers and sharecroppers to adopt new technologies.

The sharecroppers owning less than an acre of land were also beneficiaries of OB in Bira, thought some writers expressed doubts about the success of the programme in registering the names of poor sharecroppers.[58] The size of holdings of the registered *bargadars*, in Bira

---

[58] For example, Khasnobis (1981) criticized the programme on the ground that it benefited only those sharecroppers who owned or leased in a sizeable amount of land. See also Mallick (1993).

TABLE 3.21: SIZE OF HOLDINGS OF SHARECROPPERS REGISTERED
UNDER OPERATION BARGA IN BIRA

Size (in acres)	Amount of land	Percentage (in acres)
0.00-0.50	20.00	17
0.51-1.00	26.96	21
1.01-1.50	16.23	13
1.51 and above	61.10	49
Total	124.29	100

however, tell us a different story.[59] Nearly 40 per cent of registered land belong to the sharecroppers owning less than an acre (Table 3.21). Changes in the terms and conditions in the tenancy arrangement with the completion of OB also encouraged the sharecroppers of small plots to invest more. Extension of lending facilities to this group of sharecroppers helped to improve the overall situation.

Many writers have been critical about the role of the OB in influencing land relations and in raising productivity in West Bengal. Let us take a look at the arguments against the OB. Rudra (1981) pointed out that OB was a party-based struggle. Tenants belonging to the opposition parties were evicted to give place to the tenants belonging to the ruling party. Chattopadhyay (1984), whose survey included two villages in Nadia, noted that in one village (Bahirgachi) *bargadars* owing allegiance to the other or to no political or peasant organizations were unable to contact the administration and claim their due. As a result, the OB in this village was viewed by people as an exercise of CPI(M) activists for their 'camp followers'. Only 12 *bargadars* recorded their names, and most of them belonged to the CPI(M) peasant wing. Bandyopadhyay (1985) also pointed out the role of the political parties in the implementation of the OB in his survey of some villages on West Bengal.[60] He observed that in one of the villages the land-owners who were active members of the CPI(M) prevented the OB team from entering the village. The land-owners in collusion with the CPI (M) workers foiled the operation plans.

[59] See Leiten (1992), Harriss (1993) for discussion on OB's role in registering poor sharecroppers.

[60] Rudra (1981b: A 61-2, Chattopadhyay (1984: 72-95), Bandyopadhyay (1985: 13).

According to Mallick, registration was unsuccessful because

The poorer sharecroppers, with little or no land of their own, are more dependent on the landlord and therefore more afraid of being recorded as a *bargadar* for fear of eviction or simply not being able to borrow in time of need. The poorest *bargadars* are mostly from the scheduled castes and tribes who have never been able to form an effective organization of their own, and have generally been the ones left out of the *barga*-recording programme due to fear and dependence on the propertied classes. (1993: 53)

Mallick draws our attention to another side of the problem:

Under pressure from their superiors to fulfil targets, the recordings were done in a summary fashion depending often on the local Left Front cadres to select the appropriate *barga* beneficiaries. As a result, a lot of legitimate sharecroppers were not recorded and Left Front supporters were recorded in their place. (1993: 55)

The situation in Bira with regard to *barga* recording is very different from these examples. Barring a few, sharecroppers belonging to all the three categories (land-owner-cum-sharecroppers, sharecroppers and labourers-cum-sharecroppers) managed to register their name in the village between 1977 and 1979. The recording helped *bargadars* cultivation as much as 124.29 acres (Table 3.21). The sheer magnitude of *barga* recording in Bira showed that the programme rose above party consideration. The *bargadars* belonging to the CPI(M) as well as other parties, attended the evening meeting with the officials and recorded their names. Some of the *bargadars* of Hindupara who were active supporters of the Congress party were first to register their names during the OB programme. Lieten (1992) who surveyed a village in Birbhum also noted that most of the sharecroppers in the village have gone in for registration and there were no cases of hidden tenancy (replacement of sharecroppers by a more pliable tenant).[61] Bhaumik (1993) noted a high percentage of recording in the villages surveyed by him in the Midnapur district.

---

[61] However, his over all reaction was mixed as he observed that, in terms of numbers, OB succeeded quite well but, in terms of increasing income and increasing production investments, the programme had made partial success (1992: 176).

Critics like Chattopadhyay were also of the view that OB meant very little to the poor sharecroppers who lacked financial resources to cultivate land with better inputs and agricultural implements. *Panchayats* and other institutions failed in disbursing loans. It has been mentioned earlier how *bargadars* of Bira received loans to tide over the initial problems of obtaining capital for the investment in new technologies. Indebtedness among sharecroppers is a well-known phenomenon. A number of surveys have highlighted the problem of indebtedness among the sharecroppers of West Bengal. In order to meet the high cost of production, sharecroppers often borrow either from professional moneylenders or land-owners at a higher interest rate. A telling example of such borrowings can be found in Bhaduri's (1973) study. In Birbhum district, Bhaduri noticed that, on an average, for each kilogram of paddy that the *bargadar* borrows in the lean season, he pays back one and a half to two kilograms of paddy after the harvest, implying something like 50 to 100 per cent paddy rate of interest over four or five months. Bandyopadhyay (1981) reported this kind of borrowing arrangements among the *bargadars* and land-owners-cum-moneylenders in some areas in Central Bengal. Khasnobis and Chakraborty (1982) found that in some cases credit market is dominated by the non-landlord loan-givers, e.g. traders and professional moneylenders.[62] In such a situation, only institutional loan can help in breaking the traditional dependency relations between the *bargadars* and land-owners. Bandyopadhyay (1985) noted that commercial and cooperative banks offered the much needed financial support to the *bargadars* at the time of OB. He found that loans from the institutional sources which were offered to the recorded sharecroppers accounted for about 60 per cent of the total loans in the villages surveyed by him. In a recent survey, Chadha and Bhaumik (1992) observed that a greater proportion of total credit requirement of the recorded tenant is met through the institutional agencies. While nearly 73 per cent of the total credit borrowed by recorded tenants has come from institutional sources, the corresponding figure for the unrecorded tenants is 63 per cent. Thus, institutional credit became the main source of agricultural loans in the villages surveyed by them.[63] Therefore, empirical findings show the important role played by government agencies in disbursing loans to newly registered sharecroppers.

[62] Bandyopadhyay (1981: 53-68), Bhaduri (1973:12), Khasnobis and Chakraborty (1982: A 29-30).
[63] Bandhopadhyay (1985: 11-13), Chadha and Bhaumik (1992: 1093).

Two major objectives of OB, namely, conferring tenurial rights and providing financial assistance to meet cost of production have been achieved in many parts of Bengal. By and large, most of the critics of OB have ignored the problem of productive efficiency of the recorded sharecroppers. Chadha and Bhaumik (1992) who compared the performance of recorded and unrecorded tenants on sharecropped land write,

the recorded tenants report higher utilization of all inputs and gain higher productivity level on their sharecropped lands compared with the unrecorded tenants in the case of *aman* paddy. The differences are also statistically significant in most of the cases (except output per acre). ...To the extent that the recorded tenants see to perform better on their sharecropped plots compared with the performance of the unrecorded tenants on similar plots for the most important crop of our study area (*aman* paddy) and also that their performance has not been too different with respect to the other crop (*boro* paddy), our data do not lend any support to the view that launching of the OB programme has resulted in loss of production in West Bengal. ...The recorded tenants are able to extract a much larger share of total returns which surely contributes to augmentation of their incomes. Actually, the higher share of total returns accrues to them through a better exercise of their crop-sharing rights following OB. (1992: 1095)[64]

These findings would support observations made earlier with regard to the organization of production and efficiency of the recorded sharecroppers of Bira. Thus, in an area where a high percentage of land is under tenancy arrangement, OB type programme could go a long way in improving agricultural conditions. One could not agree more with Rudra when he writes,

there is a growing volume of evidence that leasing in of some amount of land is a characteristic feature of the typically enterprising farmer. The typically enterprising farmer is rarely a pure owner, that is one who cultivates only such land as is owned by him. It would seem that the typically enterprising farmer finds it to the interest of better cultivation and therefore of higher profit to lease in some parcels of land to supplement or consolidate the fragments owned by him, and if necessary leasing out some other fragments. Also increasing farm size through rented land does not get obstructed by

---

[64] Their findings are based on survey in 12 sample villages in Midnapur district. They had a total of 224 tenant household samples of whom 121 were recorded *bargadars* and 103 unrecorded.

any ceiling laws which do not apply to leased in land. (1987: 135)[65]

Even Ghatak (1995) noted that in Birbhum earlier under *kishani* arrangement, all costs other than labour were borne by the landlord and the *kishan* received only one-third.[66] Now the relatively affluent *kishans* are bearing all cultivation costs and claiming the legal share of three-fourth and, in some cases, switching to a fixed rent system. The less affluent have settled for half or two-fifth with the same proportion with the landlord. In 24 Parganas and Midnapur too, the share has gone up in general.

Citing state-level data Westergaard (1986) argued that conflict of interests between the small farmers and the sharecroppers had prompted the ruling Left Front to abandon OB. The small farmers, the support base of the CPI(M) opposed the programme because they had very little to gain from this as most of them were the lessors of land. However, state-level data would show that the OB had benefited the medium-sized peasants too. According to NSS data (26th Round), about 36 per cent of the sharecropper households, each owning between 1 and 5 acres of land accounted for about 58 per cent of the total sharecropped area. The security of tenure and the strict enforcement of the laws on tenancy brought them closer to the peasant households owning between 2.5 and 7.5 acres, consisting approximately 22 per cent of all rural households and accounting for approximately 49 per cent of the total operated area. Thus, it is difficult to subscribe to the view that the OB had adversely affected the small farmers in the state.

Small farmers and sharecroppers, especially those who combine both occupations, are now emerging as enterprising peasants in Bira. Diffusion of knowledge of agricultural innovations and the spread of new technologies have been possible for their active role in rural economy. The state with its land reforms programme and institutional support has created an ideal situation for them to modernize their production arrangements. The prospect for further growth in West Bengal agriculture now depends on this new genre of farmers and sharecroppers.

Furthermore, it has been pointed out that the OB failed to ensure the three-fourth share to the *bargadars*, which was one of the major objectives

[65] However, when it comes to the question of OB, Rudra (1982b) is of the view that registered *bargadar* suffered a set-back in terms of their income since they have mostly been able to use less modern inputs than before, that is neither from the land-owners nor from the banks.

[66] Ghatak (1995).

of the programme. Thus, Mallick writes, 'Even with respect to ensuring three-quarters crop share, OB made little progress' (1992: 139). However, Bandyopadhyay (1983) in his survey of 14 West Bengal villages noted that recorded *bargadars* received three-quarters share. It has been shown earlier how three-quarters share is adjusted between the land-owners and sharecroppers by offering 50 per cent share of the main crop only in Bira.

Studies on new technologies in agriculture and their impact on the landless labourers generally deal with three kinds of problems. First, a number of surveys have dealt with the process of pauperization in agriculturally advanced areas and swelling in the number of landless labourers. Bardhan (1970), for example, noted that in Punjab (including Haryana) the throbbing heartland of green revolution, the percentage of rural population nearly quadrupled between 1967-8. The same is true of Assam and West Bengal. In all these states the percentage of landless labourers has gone up significantly.[67] Such trends were also pointed out by Bandyopadhyay (1977), Frankel (1971) and Jose (1984) in the context of West Bengal agriculture. The nature of growth of landless labourers households in Nadia district would corroborate these findings (Table 3.14). Second, most survey findings clearly indicate deteriorating living conditions of the labourers as a result of fall in real wages. Bardhan (1970) pointed out that movement in the real wage rate for agricultural labourers had been rather disappointing. In a majority of districts, there has been a fall in the real wage rate between 1962-3 and 1967-8 (including Burdwan districts of West Bengal).[68] However, Palghat district in Kerala was an exception. According to Bardhan, unionization of agricultural labourers helped the labourers in Palghat to bargain for higher wages.[69] Gough (1984) too based her argument on similar lines. Some writers highlighted the positive gains of additional man days to

[67] Bardhan (1970: 1239).

[68] See Mallick (1993) for a detailed discussion on wage rates in West Bengal.

[69] Bardhan writes, 'This may bot be entirely unconnected with the fact that peasant organizations in Kerala are fairly strong, relative to most other parts of the country, and that in much of the period under discussion, Kerala had governments that may have been somewhat more responsive to the demands of these organizations. It seems that, in the Indian context, the bargaining strength of agricultural labourers may be at least as important a determinant of high real wage rates as the spread of technological progress in agriculture,' (1970: 1243).

undermine the importance of the fall in the real wage in technologically advanced agrarian regions.[70] The problem may be examined in little more detail with the help of village-level data.[71] Much of this section deals with these problems in the context of the technological change in Bira.

Although there existed different kinds of labour hiring arrangements in the village in the sixties, like daily wage labour, attach labour, *thika* labour with varying terms and conditions. The multiple system of labour market became obvious with the spread of new technologies. Land-owners in Bira now prefer casual labourers whose duration of contract is for a day and who receive the wage at the end of the day in cash or kind, or in both. They work for eight hours a day and enjoy freedom to work under different employers. If one takes into account the primary and secondary occupations agricultural labourers would appear as a mixed category. Broadly, there are three groups. First, 'the pure landless labourers' who do not own any land and depend entirely on wage labour to eke out their living. Fifteen households (eleven per cent) belong to this category.[72] Second, there are nine labourer households (seven per cent) who own tiny plots, less than a *bigha*, but depend primarily on wage labour. Third, there are 10 households (eight per cent) who lease in land but depend mainly on wage labour as the size of the leased in land is too small. The last two groups may be considered as 'functionally landless'. In all, one-fourth households earn their living mainly through wage labour. These households are more or less evenly distributed among the three residential areas: nine in Hindupara, eleven in Mathpara and fourteen in Musalmanpara.

In the case of Hindupara and Mathpara, the rise in the number of labourers household has taken place due to migration from the other side of the border. Those who arrived with very little capital had joined the rank of the rural labourers. However, in the case of Musalmanpara, transfer of land from the hands of the poor farmers to the better off sections of the peasantry and eviction of sharecroppers in the sixties and early seventies swelled the number of agricultural labourers. Land sales for the repayment of debt, medical expenses and social functions like marriages, accounted for pauperization in this area. Out of seven

---

[70] See Ledejinsky (1977).

[71] More discussion on this point in the next chapter.

[72] Except homestead land which they own as a result of an Act passed by the West Bengal Government to confer this right to the agricultural labourers.

sharecroppers who were evicted during the late sixties, six of them now work as agricultural labourers.

In some respects, the agricultural labourers in Bira are now better off than their counterparts in other districts in West Bengal. First of all, the movement in the wage rate between 1980 and 1988 shows an appreciable rise in the village where it increased from Rs. 6 to Rs. 18. This is consistent with the rise in the wage throughout the district between 1979-80 and 1988 (Table 3.22). In fact, comparison of district-level data show a remarkable achievement in the rise of wages in Nadia. In terms of real wage (by converting rupees into equivalent quantity of rice, as done in many studies), the labourers of Bira as well as other villages in Nadia registered some gains.[73] In 1980, Rs. 6 were worth of two kilogram of rice. In 1988, Rs. 18 got a labourer nearly four kilograms. A phenomenal rise in the wage rate has taken place in the district mainly for two reasons. The spread of new technologies, the rise in the yield rate and better price for agricultural produce have created a situation conducive for higher wages. However, this is not the only reason for higher wages. During the last one decade, the district unit of the kisan sabha had been active in mobilizing the landless for higher wages in various parts of Nadia.[74] The movement for higer wages took a new turn in 1977 when the Left Front came into power with the promise to increase wages for the labourers. The support from the top helped to intensify the struggle for higher wages by the kisan sabhas. Incidence of strikes and demonstrations became common in those cases when the land-owners paid less than the stipulated wages to the labourers. This is quite similar to the situation which Bardhan noted with regard to Palghat district in Kerala. An example may be cited to show how land-owners yield to pressure from the kisan sabha. In May 1988, at the time of sowing of *aus* paddy, some of the land-owners of Musalmanpara refused to pay Rs. 18 to wage labourers on the plea that the wage rate in the neighbouring village was Rs. 16. The agricultural labourers of Musalmanpara brought the matter into the notice of the kisan sabha which intervened and called

[73] For example, Khan (1984), van Schendel and Faraizi (1984).

[74] The term 'mobilization' is used here to refer to 'purposeful public and collective action. It is a way of creating and using political power. Those who engange in mobilizations intend to influence policy choice and implementation, asymmetrical bargaining situations or electoral choice. Mobilization is designed to generate bargaining advantages or political power on behalf of actors who believe themselves disadvantages by established institution and rules.' (Rudolph and Rudolph, 1984: 281)

TABLE 3.22: AVERAGE DAILY WAGE RATES OF AGRICULTURAL
LABOURERS IN WEST BENGAL IN 1979-80 AND 1988

Districts	1979-80	1988 (July to December)	Per cent Increase
Darjeeling	7.25	22.32	207.8
Jalpaiguri	6.95	18.37	164.3
Cooch Bihar	6.25	14.47	131.5
West Birajpur	4.95	11.12	124.6
Malda	4.35	17.57	303.9
Murshidabad	7.80	17.85	128.8
Nadia	5.40	17.98	232.9
24 Parganas (N)	7.62	17.50	129.6
24 Parganas (S)	7.62	21.07	176.5
Howrah	8.15	23.79	191.9
Hoogli	7.55	20.04	165.4
Burdwan	7.15	17.77	148.5
Birbhum	7.30	15.15	107.5
Bankura	8.00	17.62	120.2
Purulia	5.15	14.00	171.8
Midnapur	7.15	16.52 (W)	131.0

SOURCE: Government of West Bengal, *Economic Review, 1982-3* and *1989-90*.

for a strike. The land-owners realized that the only option they had was to keep their lands either fallow or pay the stipulated wages. After three days of strike, the wage was fixed at Rs. 18.

The introduction of new technologies and the rise in the cropping intensity have created additional man days for the agricultural labourers. The increase varied between 35 and 40 per cent during the *aus* cultivation, nearly 60 per cent during the *boro* season, and between 25 and 30 per cent during the *aman* season. Additional man days became indispensable for sowing, transplanting, weeding, harvesting and threshing most of the HYV crops.[75] In many parts of India, the use of machines like tractors, threshers, etc. have neutralized the gains in additional man days. The state policy against the use of machinery in agriculture has worked in favour of labourers who used to remain unemployed for a considerable period of time in a year.

[75] In some areas, state sponsored programmes like 'food-for-work' and National Rural Employment Programme helped to create additional employment opportunities. See Ghosh (1981), Mallick (1993). These programmes had not been introduced in Bira till the late eighties.

The massive programme launched in the sixties and seventies to discover surplus land and to redistribute it among poor peasants, landless labourers and sharecroppers came to an end in Bira in the mid-eighties. Not much surplus land was available for distribution as land transfers took place on a large scale right from the early sixties to avoid appropriation of surplus land by the state.[76] However, the programme to offer homestead land to the landless labourers did help in giving right to all the 34 agricultural labourers in the village households. Kisan sabha and the *panchayats* intervened on a number of occasions in the case of dispute over homestead land. For example, Satran Biswas, 35-year-old agricultural labourer, who worked in Debendra Biswas' land for about 15 years received .50 acres from the land-owner for residential purpose. After Debendra's death, his son Kamal Biswas refused Satran's claim over the land and tried to evict him. The kisan sabha and the *panchayat* intervened on behalf of Satran and called for a boycott of Kamal's land. The boycott yielded results and Satran received .50 acres of homstead land back.

Two important political institutions which have contributed a great deal in dealing with the problem of growth with equity deserve further attention. Let me comment on the role of the kisan sabhas first. An important shift in the programme of the kisan sabha took place in the late sixties when the central committee of the CPI(M) pointed out that:

the deep-rooted reformist understanding expressed itself in underestimating and underplaying the militant role of the rural proletariat and semi-proletariat in the anti-feudal struggle so for placing undue reliance on the middle and rich peasant sections; it expressed itself in the reluctance to champion the specific demands of the agricultural labourers and poor peasants, demands that were conflicting with the upper section of the peasantry and capitalist farmers; it expressed itself virtually distorting the correct concept of all peasant unity in the struggle against feudal land-lordism and building that unity based upon the middle and rich peasantry instead of building it around the rural labour and poor and mainly based upon them. (1967: 5-6)

The shift in the programme led to a new era in the sphere of peasant

[76] However, the overall performance of the state in the redistribution of surplus land is quite impressive. Till May 1985, the Government discovered 10,87,108.70 acres of land, out of which it distributed 8,04,123.25. See Government of West Bengal (1985: 39-40).

politics in West Bengal.[77] The district units of the kisan sabhas were reorganized and attempts were being made to induct more poor peasants and labourers into the kisan sabhas. Various kinds of methods were adopted by the peasant organizations to realize their demands. The district and the local committees of the WBPKS organized processions, demonstrations, strikes and gheraos from time to time. These methods were used in the case of disputes over the rights of sharecroppers or agricultural labourers. The organized protests were not confined to the boundaries of the village alone. Whenever a government official, e.g. the BDO, the JLRO or the Director of the CADC, was at fault, the kisan sabha organized demonstrations and picketing in front of government offices.[78] Blocks and district-level movements of the kisan sabha have now brought the poor farmers of the village to the arena of organized politics. An important yardstick to determine the popularity of the kisan sabha is the rapid rate of growth in the number of its members. In Nadia alone, it went up from 15,033 in 1975-6 to 1,19,920 in 1978-9. It reached nearly two lakhs in 1982-3 (Appendices I and II).

The village *panchayats* have now emerged as an alternative power structure. *Panchayat* elections are held on the basis of universal adult franchise in which each political party has a role to play. Free elections have given the poorer section an opportunity to contest and share political power. Besides carrying out developmental work like sanitation, drainage, supply of drinking water, maintenance and construction of road rehabilitation of displaced persons, the *panchayats* today play an important role in state programmes like OB, and join kisan sabhas in settling disputes over sharecropping rights or wage labour.

Panchayats played an important role in the spread of new technologies. For instance, Rao (1995) reports that under the massive World Bank funded programme, selection of tubewell sites and the beneficiaries has been done involving three tiers of the panchayat raj system, the zilla parishad, the panchayat samiti and the gram panchayat.

---

[77] The shift in the programme also inspired peasant struggles for the seizure of *benami* land its distribution among the poor throughout the late sixties. See Konar (1977), Rasul (1969) and (1974).

[78] In 1987 when CADC controlled DTW went out of order the farmers brought the matter into the notice of the CADC Director. The lackadaisical manner of functioning of the CADC in this matter triggered off protests. The kisan sabha organized demonstrations for an urgent action. It helped the farmers of Bira, the DTW was repaired shortly.

Elected members of the village *panchayat* convened a meeting of all the village residents to discuss the sites of the tubewell installation. After finalizing the location, the village *panchayat* chalked out the command area and obtained consent from the owners of the land where the tubewell was to be installed. Rao rightly notes that 'though the procedure is elaborate and time-consuming, it is probably the best way to ensure the farmers' involvement in the planning process. Besides, it ensures commitment of the farmers to the tubewell management'.[79] After installation, the panchayat samiti takes over the responsibility of maintaining them and constituting beneficiary committees for the operation and maintenance of tubewells besides fixing the water rates. The accounts were also maintained by the panchayat samiti. In this way, the local-level political bodies were involved in the introduction and management of new tubewells. While assessing the question of equity, Rao points out,

Analysis of data on water charges paid by the farmers and discussions with a cross-section of them brought out clearly that the water supplied was directly proportional to the land owned by them under the tubewell cluster. Caste and status of the farmers had no influence on the quantum of water supply. A notable feature is that equity is ensured between the head and tail-end farmers. This is achieved by supplying water for proportionately longer duration to fields away from the tubewells to compensate for seepage losses, at no extra cost.[80]

This is an unique method in dealing with the problem of water management.

Two kinds of criticism against the *panchayati* system in West Bengal are now well known. First, some writers noted negligible representation of women in the *panchayats*. This was the case in the late seventies and early eighties. In recent elections a large number of women contested for seats and won. According to Bandyopadhyay (1993), in 1993 election there were on an average 2.84 candidates per seat. There are now nearly 25,000 women members in the *panchayats*.[81] Second, *panchayati* system in West Bengal has been criticized also on the ground that the poorer strata do not have adequate representation in the local bodies. Kohli's survey (1983) in Burdwan and Midnapur districts shows a higher

[79] Rao (1995: 4118).
[80] Rao (1995: A121).
[81] Bandyopadhyay (1993: 15-21).

proportion of representation of poor marginal farmers (0-5 acres—77 per cent, 6-10 acres—19.4 per cent and more than 10 acres 2.8 per cent) in the *panchayats*.[82] Westergaard and Lieten too showed pro-poor composition of *panchayats* in West Bengal. A survey in 100 villages by Sen (1983) in 1980-1 showed that 8 per cent of the *panchayat* members belonged to the families owning land more than 7.5 acres. Those owning 5-7.5 acres or middle peasants accounted for 6.5 per cent of the total number. Families owning less than 5 acres but above 2.5 acres accounted for 31.5 per cent of the total. The rest 61 per cent of the representatives came from the whole conglomerate of the poor at the base of West Bengal's rural society.[83] However, only 7 per cent belonged to the landless agricultural labourers groups. Other writers too noted the poor representation of this group in the *panchayats*. Nevertheless, the tilt of the power balance towards the poor has come about. More recently Dasgupta (1995) showed that the 1993 *panchayat* elections gave representation to 70 per cent members from the poorer strata, 25 per cent from the middle strata and 5 per cent from the richer sections.[84]

The kisan sabha and *panchayats* have succeeded in breaking the traditional dependency relations between the owners and non-owners of land. This kind of situation thus prompted van Schendel and Faraizi to write,

The class based organization of small peasants, sharecroppers and rural labourers in West Bengal was thus successfully assisted by active leftist political parties and, at times by the state government. The main result was the disturbance of *zotdari* appropriation whose smooth operation could no longer be relied upon as pressure mounted on the *jotdars* to adopt to the changing rural power structure. (1984: 121)

In West Bengal, kisan sabhas and *gram panchayats* by mobilizing the rural poor prevented some of the negative effects of technological growth, e.g. eviction of sharecroppers, displacement of small cultivators who lacked resources for the use of new technology and payment of insufficient wage to the agricultural labourers. Many areas in India where green revolution has been successful face the complex problem of balancing growth with equity. It has been an Indian experience that in

[82] Bandyopadhyay (1993: 18-21).
[83] Sen (1983: 3-9).
[84] Dasgupta (1995: 2691-702).

the battle between growth and equity, the former prevails over the latter. However, situations in West Bengal present an alternative scenario. It shows how state intervention and reactivization of local-level political institutions can ensure growth with equity. The *bargadars*, the small farmers and agricultural labourers are not in the receiving ends in the state anymore. They are the vangurds of agrarian change which is sweeping through rural West Bengal today.

CHAPTER FOUR

Bangladesh: The New Technology and Agrarian Change

4.1 THE LAND PROBLEM

In January 1987, Bangladesh had 104 million inhabitants who lived on a territory of 55,600 square miles or 1,44,000 square kilometres. It became the ninth most populous country in the world. In 1985-6, Bangladesh's per capita income was 4,400 *Taka* per annum, which was equivalent to US $147. However, the poorest 40 per cent of Bangladesh had a substantially low per capita income, approximately 2450 *Taka* or $ 82.[1] Other indicatiors may also be taken into account to get an idea about the poverty situation in Bangladesh. In the eighties, the per capita daily consumption of food fluctuated around 2,000 calories. In 1983-4, about 37 per cent of Bangladesh's population consumed less than 1,800 calories per capita per day, far less than the minimum standard requirement. Low consumption of food over a long period of time has led to other problems. About 9 per cent of Bangladesh's children suffered from some degree of malnutrition. Infant mortality rate was particularly high as 122 of every thousand children born were expected to die before one year. The 1981 census showed that only 29 per cent of the adults (over 15) were literate.

Like many developing countries, agriculture is the most important sector in the national economy of Bangladesh today. A high percentage of population (nearly 89 per cent) lives in the rural areas and agriculture's share of the gross domestic product is around 57 per cent.[2] In contrast, West Bengal has a better track record. In 1981, West Bengal's population was 54.5 million and it had an over all per capita income of $139. The percentage of population living in rural areas was only 74 and labour force engaged in agriculture remained 55 per cent. Compared to

---

[1] Khan and Hossain (1989: 5).
[2] *Bangladesh Statistical Handbook, 1985.*

TABLE 4.1: SOME GENERAL SOCIO-ECONOMIC INDICATORS OF DEVELOPMENT IN BANGLADESH AND WEST BENGAL

Indicators	Bangladesh	West Bengal
Total Area (sq miles)	55,598	34,214
Population (1985) (in million)	100.5	59.07
Density of Population (1985, per sq mile)	1806	1726
Population Growth Rate (1971-81, per cent per annum)	2.6	2.3
Rural Population as Percentage of Total Population (1981)	84.33	73.53
Literacy (1981) (per cent)	20.2	40.94
Per capita GDP (1986-7) (in US $)	150	215
Percentage of Population below Poverty Line (1980)	80	60

SOURCE: Siddiqui *et al.* (1988).

Bangladesh infant mortality rate was lower and the literacy rate (around 35 per cent) was particularly high in West Bengal (see Table 4.1).

In Bangladesh land reform measures were undertaken by the erstwhile Pakistan Government right from the early fifties. The East Bengal State Acquisition and Tenancy Act (EBSATA) of 1950 abolished the *zamindari* land tenure system and all kinds of intermediary interest between the state and the cultivator. Unlike West Bengal, the Act of 1950 enabled the former rent receiving land-owners in East Bengal not only to retain the major and most productive segments of their traditional holdings but also to exercise their customary rights. Initially the ceiling on holdings was 100 standard *bighas* (approximately 33 acres), subsequently it was raised to 375 standard *bighas* (approximately 125 acres) by the East Pakistan Ordinance of 1961. In 1972, the ceiling limit was reduced to 100 *bighas* again.[3] However, for various reasons the state had very little land at its disposal for redistribution among the poor peasants. Therefore, one of the basic objectives of land reforms, i.e. confiscation of surplus land and its redistribution among the poor, had not been successful in Bangladesh.

Land reforms programme had nothing to offer to protect the tenurial rights of the sharecroppers. The EBSATA of 1950 prohibited the acquisition of occupancy rights by sharecroppers and noted that persons holding land under another person and paying a share of the produce to that person would be classified as *bargadars* and the share of the produce payable by such *bargadars* would not be considered as rent within the meaning of the Act. Thus, the sharecroppers were deprived of their tenurial rights and other protection under the law. The land policies of the East Pakistan Government gradually led to the process of pauperization in the countryside and the crisis reached its peak at the time of liberation war in 1971 when the economy was completely shattered as a result of military atrocities.

The land problem attracted attention of the policy makers of the newly independent state as landlessness became acute in the seventies. In 1972, the Awami League Government promulgated several presidential orders to change the existing land reform legislations. As mentioned earlier they reduced the family ceiling once again to 100 *bighas*, made provisions for the redistribution of surplus lands among the landless and abolished land tax on holdings below 25 *bighas* (8.3 acres). The government also abolished *'ijaradari'* with respect to the management of *'sairat mahal'* or government landed property, e.g. *hats* and *bazars*, water bodies, ferries, mines, minerals, etc. However, due to political instability and acute economic crises, the government achieved very little in solving the land problem. New pieces of legislation were adopted again in 1984 to make land reforms programme more effective. This time Bangladesh Land Reforms Ordinance, 1984 was introduced. Ceiling provisions remained unaffected. However, for the first time steps were taken to protect tenurial security of the sharecroppers and to fix minimum wage for agricultural labourers. The efficacy of these measures are examined later in this chapter.

Although progress with regard to implementation of land reforms programme has been extremely tardy, some changes in the landholding size are clearly noticeable. For example, Khan and Hossain (1989) by using Land Occupancy Survey and Agricultural Census data compared

---

[3] Bangladesh Landholding Limitation Order, 1972.

the land size distribution between the 1978 and 1983-4 period. They showed a tendency towards persistence of small farms, less than 2.49 acres. Bhaduri, Rahman and Arn (1986) too noted a trend towards persistence of small holdings in rural Bangladesh. In support of their arguments for the persistence of small farms, the authors generated a measure of present landholdings operationalized as the ratio between land inherited and current landholdings. The households were grouped into four landholding categories and compared by landholding stability. The authors observed that between 39.0 and 52.2 per cent of all households in each landholding category showed little or no change in the amount of land owned. Outside income, especially from agricultural employment and leasing in of land, were some of the factors accounting for stabilization of land ownership among the small land-owners. The theory of the persistence of small farmers has been criticized by Feldman and McCarthy (1987), Khan (1987), Pandian (1987) on several counts. Some of the most pertinent points are that it is quite difficult to accept the view that wage labour provides an additional income opportunity for the small holders in a situation where labour market is plagued by a very high rate of unemployment. Secondly, leasing in of land seldom helps small owners in a situation where terms and conditions do not favour the lessees at all. Moreover, persistence or polarization cannot be measured by changes within a single generation. Even Land Occupancy Survey and Agricultural Census data do show a tendency towards persistence of small farms at the national level. Like West Bengal, in Bangladesh too small farms have come into prominence.

Although no reliable figure is available regarding the extent of tenancy, especially sharecropping tenancy in Bangladesh, many writers belive that about one-third land is under tenancy arrangement.[4] The 1976 Pilot Agricultural Census of Bangladesh reported 41.6 per cent of farm households as either tenants or owners-cum-tenants. Jannuzi and Peach (1980) pointed out that the extent of tenancy remained relatively stable over the past two decades. The 1960 Census of Agriculture reported 39.2 per cent land was under sharecropping and according to the 1967 Master Survey of Agriculture it was 33.5 per cent.

Adverse terms and conditions of sharecropping arrangements (with wide variations from district to district, have not been conducive to agricultural growth. Most tenants do not remain on the same land for a long time. In general, input costs are exclusively borne by the tenants

[4] Boyce (1987), van Schendel (1991).

and the division of crop takes place on a 50 : 50 basis, in some cases land-owners' share exceed 50 per cent. Possibilities for adoption of new technologies by the tenants under such conditions are extremely remote.

The land problem has taken a new turn in recent times with the steep rise in the number of agricultural landless labourers, from 1.5 million in 1951 to 2.47 million in 1961. The number went up to 4.54 million in 1977 and then on to 5.11 million in the 1983-4 period.[5] Abdullah et al. (1976) estimated the changes in landlessness in rural Bangladesh between 1960 and 1981 on the basis of 1960 and 1981 agricultural census and 1961 population census data. They noted that between 1960 and 1981, there was an increase of 42.5 per cent in the number of landless labourers (a growth rate of 2 per cent per annum). In absolute number, there was an increase of landless households from 3.07 million to 4.34 million. Districts like Noakhali, Comilla, Jessore, Pabna, Faridpur and Mymensigh experienced the highest growth rate while Dhaka, Chittagong, Sylhet, Bogra and Bakerganj had a moderate rate of growth. Nothing has been done through the land reforms programme to improve the economic condition of rural landless labourers. Unlike in West Bengal, the benefits of land redistribution programme have not reached the landless agricultural labourers.

4.2 THE NEW TECHNOLOGY IN AGRICULTURE

The Bangladesh Government made efforts to build up an infrastructure for irrigation from the mid-seventies. A number of projects were undertaken for the development of surface and under-water irrigation. Lift pumps, DTWs and STWs were imported and sold out among the farmers at a subsidized rates. Funds were allocated for the development of canal irrigation. The first major ground water irrigation project, the Ganges-Kobadak Project (GKP), received substantial financial assistance for its expansion. Along with this, the Government of Bangladesh spent a great deal to increase the domestic production of fertilizers. It undertook special programmes to popularize HYVs. Many new varieties were introduced in place of the traditional varieties both for cereal and non-cereal crops. Pesticides were made available at a subsidized rate too. As a result of the spread of new technologies, the yield rate of major crops improved. The improvement was

[5] Agricultural Census.

particularly noticeable in the production of cereal crops, wheat and the winter rice. The nature of rise in the food production may be examined later in this section, but first let us consider the nature of growth of new technologies in Bangladesh agriculture.[6]

The groundwork for the development of modern irrigation infrastructure began in the late sixties. In 1969, mechanical irrigation was used in about 420,000 acres and indigenous irrigation in about 1 million acres.[7] At this time, about 11,000 pumps were utilized. In 1970, the government decided to raise the number of pumps from 11,000 to 19,000 in order to mechanically irrigate one million acres. Throughout the seventies, the Water and Power Development Authority (WAPDA) attempted to extend these areas further by opening up new canals for surface-water irrigation. DTWs and STWs were also installed in a large number. As a result, in the early seventies the Bangladesh Government managed to bring 9 per cent of the total cropped area under irrigation.[8]

The modern irrigation infrastructure developed at a rapid rate between 1976 and 1984. During this period, the government spent 42 per cent of its rural development expenditure on irrigation and flood control. A new Bangladesh Water Development Board (BWDB) was established which severed its link with the power sector and launched a number of projects for surface and underground water irrigation. The BWDB extended subsidies for private ownership of LLPs, DTWs and STWs. The number of LLPs with a capacity of 1-2 cubic feet per second rose from 3,000 in 1965-6 to about 35,000 in the late seventies.[9] In 1978-9, the government started selling DTWs to groups and individuals at a subsidy of about 70-80 per cent of the actual cost. As a result, the number of DTWs increased from 800 in 1970-1 to 4,500 in 1976-7 and then to 16,700 by 1984-5.[10] Steps were undertaken to popularize small capacity (less than 0.5 cubic feet per second) STWs. The sale of STWs picked up significantly during the 1979-83 period as the

---

[6] Some issues relating to the growth of new technologies have been examined by Boyce (1987), Faidley (1976), Khan and Hossain (1989), Quasem (1978 and 1979), Rahman (1964 and 1967), Smith (1975), Thomas (1975).

[7] Hamid *et al.* (1978).

[8] Boyce (1987: 173).

[9] Boyce (1987: 176).

[10] Boyce (1987: 179-80).

Bangladesh Krishi Bank extended loans to farmers to purchase STWs. According to one estimate, there were 170,000 STWs in the country in the mid-eighties.[11] As a result of all these efforts, the total irrigated area increased from 10 per cent in 1969 to 25.7 per cent in 1984-5.[12]

However, there were hurdles with the ground-water irrigation expansion programme. A large number of operational problems with regard to LLPs, DTWs and STWs began to crop up. It was difficult to get skilled manpower to run the machines. Very few had the first hand knowledge to run the imported pumps. Moreover, parts of these machines were also not available in the market. As a result, a large number of machines were discarded for lack of repair.[13] Besides this, in some cases no attempt was made to survey the area to locate the underground water level before installing DTWs. Had these loopholes been plugged on time. Bangladesh could have achieved more in developing irrigation facilities.

The area sown with HYV rice and wheat was negligible in 1971 when Bangladesh achieved independence. However, the land under modern varieties of seeds increased to 14 per cent of the cropped area by 1976-7 and to one-third of the area by 1986-7. Expansion of area under HYV seeds showed marked improvement since the late sixties as a result of large scale import of HYVs from the International Rice Research Institute (IRRI) in the Philippines and the Indian Council of Agricultural Research (ICAR). Since its inception in 1970, the Bangladesh Rice Research Institute (BRRI) too had brought out different types of HYVs. By 1985 HYV, were used in nearly one-third of the cereal area and 97 per cent of wheat producing land. With regard to rice, 78 per cent of *boro*, 16 per cent *aus* and 20 per cent *aman* were covered under HYVs.[14] According to official estimates, the share of HYV rice in total acreage was only 15.5 per cent during the seventies, this doubled during the eighties and claimed almost half of total rice acreage in the early nineties. As a result, the contribution of HYV rice in total rice production more than doubled from about 30 per cent during the seventies to about 64 per cent in the early nineties.

The use of irrigation and HYVs in the late seventies and early eighties led to higher consumption of fertilizers which increased from less than

[11] Hossain (1989: 27-8).

[12] Boyce (1987: 178).

[13] Jansen (1979) commentéd on this problems in greater detail.

[14] Hossain (1989: 35).

2000 metric tons of nutrients in 1950-3 to about 11,000 metric tons in 1959-60.[15] In 1970-1, the aggregate consumption went up to 145,000 metric tons. There was a downward trend in the use of fertilizers in the early seventies due to the disturbance at the time of the liberation war. However, fertilizer consumption went up again to 356,000 metric tons in 1977-8.[16] In order to increase the domestic supply of fertilizer, urea plants were constructed at Fenchuganj and Ghorasal and a complex for producing TSP came up at Chittagong. In the early eighties, virtually all HYV *boro*, HYV transplanted *aus* and tobacco as well as 70 to 90 per cent of plots sown with HYV broadcast *aus*, HYV, *aman*, wheat, and sugarcane received fertilizers.

The spread of irrigation, HYV seeds and fertilizers in Bangladesh between 1976-7 and 1986-7 show the complementarity of three major inputs (Table 4.2). A rise in irrigation acreage led to an increase in the use of HYVs and fertilizers. Thus, like West Bengal, here too irrigation played the key role. The increased use of HYVs, fertilizers and irrigation contributed towards two-third increase in crop output during the 1975-85 period.[17]

Inter-district variations in the use of new technologies in agriculture could be noticed in Bangladesh too. New technologies made headway especially in the districts like Chittagong, Chittagong Hill Tracts, Bogra, Comilla and Kushtia. These districts had high irrigation intensity and high fertilizer and HYV seeds intake. These areas formed the 'green revolution' belts of Bangladesh. In the late sixties and early seventies, Sylhet and Chittagong ranked first two in the use of irrigation. From the late seventies, however, a substantial grwoth in irrigation took place in the districts like Dhaka and Kushtia. In the 1956-61 period, Kushtia had only 0.1 irrigated gross cropped area which increased to 4.7 in 1969-70 and then to 26.8 in 1976-8.[18] The growth was particularly significant in view of the fact that about 64.6 per cent of land in Kushtia belonged to the category of 'high land'.[19] To bring such a sizeable

[15] Although chemical fertilizers have been more in use since the early fifties, they were used primarily in tea gardens and government experimental farms.

[16] Hossain (1989: 12).

[17] Hossain (1989: 46).

[18] Boyce (1987: 173-4).

[19] A high land is an area which normally does not go under water at any time of the year and is solely dependent on rain and artificial irrigation for cultivation.

TABLE 4.2: THE SPREAD OF HYVS, FERTILIZERS AND IRRIGATION IN
BANGLADESH BETWEEN 1976-7 AND 1986-7

Year	Percentage of Rice and Wheat Area Under HYV	Fertilizer Sales per unit of Cropped Land (kg of nutrient per hectare)	Area Irrigated Mechanically as a Percentage of Cultivated Land
1976-7	14.2	19.8	8.5
1977-8	16.6	26.9	9.6
1978-9	19.4	27.4	10.0
1979-80	22.7	30.9	11.0
1980-1	25.4	31.6	12.2
1981-2	25.8	29.9	13.3
1982-3	28.2	33.8	15.3
1983-4	28.3	39.8	17.0
1984-5	31.5	45.3	19.7
1985-6	31.0	40.0	20.0
1986-7	33.2	45.8	N.A.

SOURCES: *Bangladesh Statistical Yearbook* and *Monthly Statistics Bulletin*.

proportion of high land under irrigation had been possible due to the expansion of the surface-water irrigation under the GKP. In 1976-7, the irrigation intensity in Kushtia went up to 1.37, highest in the country, whereas national average remained at 1.11 at this time.[20]

During the 1977-84 period, Chittagong and Comilla topped in the use of fertilizers. In 1978-80, fertilizer intensity or commodity kg per hectare per crop was 144.0 in Chittagong, 133.3 in Comilla, 115.8 in Bogra and 107.0 in Kushtia. During this time, the national average was only 60.8. In Kushtia, fertilizer intensity increased from 22.1 in 1969-70 to 29.7 in 1978-80. The districts where irrigation became popular in the early seventies, e.g. Chittagong, Bogra, Comilla, and Kushtia, showed an upward trend in the use of HYVs. Right from the late seventies, the HYV intensity or percentage area under HYVs in Kushtia was above the national average. In 1977-8, for *aman* crop, the HYV intensity in Kushtia was 16.4 whereas the national average was only 6.4. Similarly, for *aus* crop, the HYV intensity was 10.5 whereas the national average was 8.0. Data on other crops, e.g. *boro*, wheat, tobacco and sugarcane showed similar trends.

[20] Here irrigation intensity is equal to gross irrigated area divided by net irrigated area.

As a result of changes in the use of new technology, rice production which was 11.5 million tons during the end of the sixties went up to 15.7 million tons in the early seventies. The trend rate of growth during the 1973-87 period was estimated at 2.2 per cent per year and the growth took place largely due to an expansion of area (37 per cent per year) under irrigated *boro* rice and an increase in yield of *boro* (2.0 per cent per year) and *aman* rice (1.3 per cent per year). The cereal production went up especially for an increase in area (14 per cent per year) and yield (5.2 per cent per year) of wheat. The area under wheat increased from only 123,000 ha in 1973-4 to 677,000 ha by 1984-5, and production increased from 111,000 tons to 1.46 million tons.[21] However, according to Khan and Hossain (1989), the recent growth in cereal production was achieved at the expense of non-cereal food crops as the area sown under oil seeds, pulses and spices declined in absolute terms from the pre-Independence levels largely due to reallocation of land to wheat and *boro* rice.[22] Availability of irrigation, HYVs and fertilizers made cultivation of rice and wheat more profitable. For example, average yield rate (in tons per hectare) of *aman* rice in 1968-71 was 1.14 which increased to 1.40 in 1984-7 leading to an overall change of about 23 per cent. In the case of *boro*, it increased from 2.03 in 1968-71 to 2.20 in 1984-7, showing 21 per cent change. And in the case of wheat, it increased from 0.85 in 1968-71 to 2.00 in the 1984-7 period. The overall percentage increase was 135.[23] The production of jute had been erratic largely due to fluctuations in market price. Among other crops, the yield rate of tea, potato and tobacco also rose during the above-mentioned period. Therefore, the spread of new technologies in agriculture led to an increase in crop production in some districts where irrigation, HYVs and fertilizer use was high.

New technologies had spread especially in districts which were selected for intensive rural development programme. For instance, the district Comilla was specifically chosen for the purpose of intensive cultivation. In 1960, a large scale rural development programme was launched in Comilla and a research institute was established. In the mid-seventies, the institute was renamed as the Bangladesh Academy for Rural Development (BARD).[24] The introduction of DTWs by BARD

[21] Boyce (1987: 172-6).

[22] Khan and Hossain (1989: 43).

[23] Khan and Hossain (1989: 44).

[24] It was called East Pakistan Academy for Village Development earlier.

helped to increase the irrigation intensity. In the earlier days, rice cultivation during the *rabi* season had not been possible for lack of water, DTWs made *boro* rice cultivation popular in the district. BARDs efforts to introduce DTWs, HYVs and fertilizers increased the cropping intensity as well as yield rates of some of the major crops. However, a district like Kushtia advanced agriculturally due to an expansion of the surface-water irrigation project at the confluence of the Ganges-Kobadak rivers. The project was designed to provide canal water for two *kharif* crops only, full irrigation for the first *kharif* and supplementing rain water during the second *kharif* season. There was also a plan to supply water during the dry season between November and April. The GKP provided an ideal infrastructure for the agricultural growth in the district.

4.3 AGRARIAN CHANGE IN KUSHTIA

Since Partition in 1947 the pace of growth in agriculture has remained tardy in Kushtia. It was one of the backward districts of the then East Pakistan in terms of both agriculture and industrial growth. The few jute and textile mills which were the chief source of employment were on the verge of collapse. When the prospects for industrial and agricultural growth were beginning to look bleak, a grandiose project for the spread of irrigation was introduced in the mid-fifties to save it from further disaster. The project aimed at using river water of the Ganges (or the Padma as it is known in East Bengal) and the Kobadak for the purpose of irrigation in over two-third cultivable areas in Kushtia and some areas in Jessore. In 1969-70, the first phase of expansion of the GKP came into an end at a cost of 23 crore *Taka*. It covered an area of 210 thousand acres of land in the districts of Kushtia and Jessore. Five *thanas* in Kushtia came under its cammand, namely Bheramara, Mirpur, Kushtia, Kumarkhali and Khoksha, and it covered 27 union *parishads* and 293 villages. In Jessore, two *thanas*, namely Sailkupa and Sreepur which had 17 union *parishads* and 284 villages were also covered under the GKP. The project head-quarters was located at Kushtia town with its offtake headworks at Bheramera on the right bank of the Padma (see Map 11).[25]

[25] The total cost for the GK Project was estimated at US $ 49.3 million of which 37 million came as an Asian Development Bank loan and $ 10.9 million was received from the Government of Bangladesh. The UNDP offered to cover the cost of staff training, consultancy services and for technical assistance.

At the initial stage, a large number of factors were favourable for the growth of the GKP. Plenty of water was available in the Padma river throughout the year. The flow of water of the river Ganges had not been interrupted then.[26] The problem of river erosion was sorted out by the construction of the Hardinge Bridge. The point at Bheramera was particularly suitable for diversion of water from the Ganges through intake channels for irrigation as far as to Khulna, a coastal district which encountered saline water inundation problem for several decades. This was also an ideal site for the generation of hydro-electricity. The control in the flow of river water as a result of the construction of the Hardinge Bridge helped irrigation and electricity generation programme.

The GKP was completed in two phases. In the first phase, an infrastructure with a command area of some 42,000 ha was completed between 1955 and 1972. The second phase which began in the early seventies increased the irrigated acreage by further 83,000 ha. The scheme was operated as well as maintained by the WAPDA and BWDB during these two phases. The first phase helped the completion of the main irrigation canal of total length of 45.64 miles, the secondary canals of 132.75 miles and tertiary canals of 298 miles. The second phase succeeded in adding 64.90 miles to the second main canal. Irrigation had spread to agricultural fields through a network of canals consisting of the main, secondary, tertiary, field and plot channels (see Map 11).

The year-wise irrigation progress (in crop acreage) for three seasons, *kharif* I (coinciding with the cultivation of *aman*) *kharif* II (coinciding with the cultivation of *aus*) and *rabi* can be seen in Table 4.3. The GKPs performance in *kharif* II had been better than *kharif* I. Year-wise progress of irrigated acreage under the GKP since 1969-70 shows that except in early and late seventies, the increase in the acreage under *kharif* I has been more or less steady. Since the early seventies, the irrigated acreage increase under *kharif* II has also been steady except twice when a decrease in the percentage could be noticed. On two occasions, irrigated acreage under *rabi* registered phenomenal rise. Overall changes in the acreage under irrigation show a net gain in spite of occasional fall in some years. Attempts were made to provide water during the *rabi* season only on four occasions in the early eighties. The programme to supply water during the *rabi* season had to be curtailed

---

[26] The construction of Farakka Barrage in West Bengal affected the flow of river water considerably and this became a source of conflict between India and Bangladesh.

TABLE 4.3: YEAR-WISE PROGRESS OF IRRIGATED ACREAGE
UNDER THE GKP SINCE 1969-70

Year	*Kharif* I	Percentage increase	*Kharif* II	Percentage increase	*Rabi*
1969-70	16,080		66,788		
1970-1	6,510	-147	67,454	-0.9	
1971-72	6,401	-1.7	46,461	-45.1	
1972-73	27,644	331	51,876	11.6	
1973-74	34,573	25	53,822	3.7	
1974-75	35,874	3.7	51,449	4.6	
1975-76	36,596	1.9	53,362	3.7	
1976-77	42,126	15.1	54,202	1.5	1,000
1977-78	39,419	-6.8	64,607	19.1	2,043
1978-79	28,328	-39.1	66,224	2.5	
1979-80	25,322	-11.8	71,665	8.2	
1980-81	41,180	62.6	76,706	7.0	6,060
1981-82	42,356	2.8	82,109	7.0	5,771
1982-83	49,078	15.8	83,292	1.4	
1983-84	45,141	-8.7	85,308	2.4	
1984-85	46,033	1.9	82,408	-3.5	
1985-86	37,095	-24	92,140	11.8	
1986-87	41,130	10.8	90,175	-2.1	
1987-88	39,032	5.3	91,523	1.4	

Source: GK Project Report, 1987-8.

because of insufficient flow of water in the Padma river as a sequel to the regulation of water in the Farakka Barrage in West Bengal. The project did fulfil the primary objective in ensuring supply of water during the *kharif* seasons, especially to help cultivation of two major crops, *aus* and *aman*. It also protected farmers from erratic rainfall and drought.

One can get a fairly clear idea about the impact of GKP on the use of HYVs, fertilizers, crop productivity, cropping intensity, employment and income opportunities from the farm management survey reports conducted in the GKP command area between 1969-70 and 1979-80. A marked improvement could be noticed in the use of HYV seeds, fertilizers and pesticides (Tables 4.4 and 4.5) in the land under the control of the GKP. HYV seeds including IR-8, IR-20, IR-176, etc., were planted in *aus*, *aman* and *boro* seasons. The number of farmers using HYVs increased from 1,698 in 1969-70 to 36,430 in 1974-5 and to 65,912 in 1979-80. Similar upward trend was noticed in the use of fertilizers and pesticides. The use of urea, TSP and MP fertilizers also showed significant improvement (Tables 4.4 and 4.5).

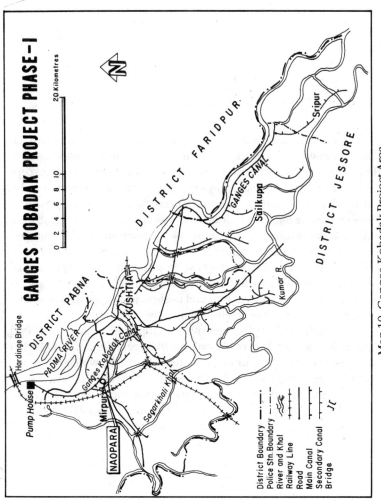

Map 10. Ganges-Kobadak Project Area.

GROWTH WITH EQUITY

TABLE 4.4: PROGRESS IN THE USE OF HYV SEEDS IN
THE GKP KUSHTIA UNIT

Year	Kharif I	Kharif II	HYV used in Maunds Total
1969-70	1,680	18	1,698
1974-5	22,975	13,445	36,430
1979-80	29,912	36,000	65,912
1984-5	40,851	79,262	1,20,113

SOURCE: BWDB, Agro-Economic Evaluation Report (GKP Project Phase I), 1982.

Irrigation facilities ensured production of at least two crops in Kushtia. During the *kharif* I season, farmers now grow wheat besides *aus* rice. During the pre-project period, it was not possible to grow crop (except mixed *aman* and sugarcane) in some areas. With the inception of the GKP, HYV and LT *aman* were introduced during the *kharif* II period. New crops were introduced in the *rabi* season, e.g. HYV wheat, tobacco, oil seeds, potato and garlic. In most cases, farmers in the GK command area are now producing either HYV *aus* or HYV *aman* and pulses or tobacco (Chart 4.1). During the post-project period, the expansion of acreage under HYV *aus* and *aman* is particularly significant. A comparison of cropping pattern in pre- and post-project periods points out a clear rise in the cropping intensity during the later period.

Along with the cropping intensity, the cropping acreage of irrigated land also increased. In 1969-70, only 66,788 acres in *kharif* I and 16,080 acres in *kharif* II were irrigated by the GK canals, which increased to 91,706 in *kharif* I and 18,500 in *kharif* II in 1988-9. The increase of acreage under mixed *aus*, jute, sugarcane and vagetables were particularly phenomenal during the *kharif* I period. During the *kharif* II period, the increase of acreage under broadcast *aman*, mixed *aman*, pulses, oil

TABLE 4.5: USE OF FERTILIZER IN THE GK COMMAND AREA

Fertilizer Use (in tons)	1969-70	1974-5	1979-80
1. Urea	595	2,598	4,564
2. TSP	510	1,593	3,182
3. MP	254	1,422	1,498

SOURCE: BWDB, Agro-Economic Evaluation Report (GK Project Phase), 1982.

CHART 4.1: CROPPING PATTERN IN THE PRE- AND
POST-PROJECT PERIODS, GKP, KUSHTIA

	Pre-Project			Post-Project	
Kharif I	*Kharif* II	*Rabi*	*Kharif* I	*Kharif* II	*Rabi*
Aus (mixed)	—	Pulses/Oil	HYV-T *Aus*	HYV-T *Aman*	Pulses
B *Aus*	—	Pulses/	—	Early HYV	Pulses/
Wheat		T *Aman*	T *Aman*	Oil Seeds	
Jute	—	Pulses/	—	HYV-T *Aman*	HYV
		Wheat			Wheat
Aman	Mixed	Pulses/	HYV-T *Aus*	LT *Aman*	Pulses
(mixed)	*Aman*	Wheat	Pulses		
B *Aman*	—	Pulses/	Jute/	HYV	Tobacco
		Wheat	B *Aus*	T *Aman*	
Sugarcane	Sugarcane	Sugarcane	Sugarcane	Sugarcane	Sugarcane

SOURCE: BWDB, Report, Kushtia Unit 1.

seeds and vegetables was significant too (Table 4.6). It was expected that the cropping intensity could be raised from 125 per cent to 250 per cent. However, the actual cropping intensity in 1977-8 remained around 141 per cent. The increase in area under cultivation of broadcast and HYV *aus* during the 1987-8 *kharif* I period is phenomenal, so is the increase in the cultivation of broadcast and HYV *aman* during the *kharif* II period in the same year. Among the *rabi* crops, increase in the acreage under pulses, and oil seeds is significant (Table 4.6). The figures provided by the FMSRs show a significant rise in the yield of broadcast *aus* and vegetables during the *kharif* I period and HYV *aman*, pulses and vegetables during the *kharif* II period.[27] However, a drop in the total

[27] The impact of the GKP on crop yields especially yields of three rice crops namely *aman* (IR 20), Local T and B *aman* has been studied by Hamid *et al.* (1978). The survey was carried out in four *thanas* under the GKP. A comparison of pre-project and post-project figures in their survey showed that before the inception of the project, the local *aman* crop yield rate was 13 *maunds* per acre. During the post-project period, the productivity of the local *aman* increased to 47 *maunds* per acre. Similarly, the productivity of local T *aman* increased to 27 *maunds* per acre on an average, which meant an increase of 14 *maunds* in an acre. Broadcast *aman* too showed an increase of 7 *maunds* per acre. Therefore, the overall impact of the GKP on crop yields was positive.

yields of some crops like mixed *aus*, sugarcane in the *kharif* I and broadcast *aman* and mixed *aman* in the *kharif* II period can be noticed. Thus, irrigation expansion led to the rise in the acreage under HYVs, and inputs and correspondingly a steep rise in the food production.

The FMSRs dealt with two other problems. Firstly, the surveys examined the cost of production of essential inputs in the GKP command area and actual profit earned by the farmers. Secondly, the FMSRs examined the impact of the irrigation project on the farm size. During phase I when the project was in its peak in 1977-8, farmers managed to

TABLE 4.6: AREA COVERED, YIELD OF *KHARIF* I AND II AND *RABI* CROPS
IN THE GK COMMAND AREA IN 1987-8 AND PRE-PROJECT PERIOD

Name of the Crops	Area Covered (in acres)		Total Yield (in *maunds*)	
	1987-8	Pre-Project	1987-8	Pre-Project
KHARIF I				
Broadcast *aus*	38,067	7,584	6,85,206	92,525
Mixed *aus*	5,900	32,232	59,000	3,93,230
LIV *aus*	847	NA	16,093	NA
HYV *aus*	36,540	NA	14,98,140	NA
Jute	10,434	12,000	1,66,944	1,56,000
Sugarcane	6,568	4,375	2,69,200	10,93,750
Vegetables	1,947	350	97,350	17,500
Others	4,724	3,125	NA	NA
KHARIF II				
Broadcast *aman*	4,158	22,752	62,370	2,82,125
Mixed *aman*	5,900	32,232	76,700	4,19,016
LIV *aman*	3,605	NA	90,125	NA
HYV *aman*	79,303	NA	38,06,544	NA
Others	1,470	NA	NA	NA
RABI				
LIV Wheat	6,000	NA	30,600	
HYV Wheat	11,991	NA	2,15,838	NA
Local *Boro*	NA	NA	NA	NA
HYV *Boro*	NA	NA	NA	NA
Tobacco	NA	770	9,240	NA
Pulses	NA	48,865	5,86,380	1,20,000
Oil seeds	NA	6,927	69,270	19,860
Vegetables	NA	1,926	1,15,560	30,250
Others	NA	1,049	NA	NA

SOURCE: BWDB, Agro-Economic Evaluation Report (GK Project Phase I), 1982.

have an overall additional benefit worth 12.45 crores *taka* in the entire project area. Survey data show that the captial investment on seeds, fertilizers, insecticides, bullocks and labour on crops like HYV cereals, jute, sugarcane in the GKP area was not too high for the farmers. Data on investment on major crops in irrigated and non-irrigated areas would reveal that investment in irrigated areas was marginally high (Table 4.7). The FMSRs data on the per acre labour cost on irrigated and non-irrigated land show that investment on labour is higher on the irrigated land. A higher cost of labour is associated with the higher demand for labour. Farmers who are producing HYV crops require at least two times more labour than traditional variety. The development of new technologies thus created additional employment opportunities in the district.

The FMSR data on the farm size give us an idea about the changing land holding structure in the GKP command area. In the 1981-2 period, the highest percentage of farm land was found in the size group between 2.00 and 5.99 acres. Those who belonged to the farm size of less than 2.00 acres owned only 7.44 per cent of total farm land (Table 4.8). The concentration of farm land in the size group 10.00 acres and above was 24.40 per cent, much higher than the national average.[28] This shows a

TABLE 4.7: PER ACRE CAPITAL INVESTMENT ON SEEDS, FERTILIZERS, PESTICIDES AND HIRED LABOUR IN IRRIGATED AND UNIRRIGATED AREAS IN KUSHTIA (*in Takas*)

Crops	Capital Investment on various items							
	Seeds		Fertilizer		Pesticides		Hired Labour	
	Irrig.	Non Irrig.	Irrig.	Non Irrig.	Irrig.	Non Irrig.	Irrig.	Non Irrig.
HYV *Aman*	72.00	110.00	897.38	869.52	75.85	64.00	866.00	520.80
HYV *Aus*	64.00	102.00	810.84	744.14	74.59	—	853.20	621.80
Jute	33.00	42.00	571.56	695.00	65.15	186.69	935.20	792.80
Sugarcane	720.30	709.15	1460.88	1015.16	381.71	82.22	1728.00	974.40
Tobacco	234.75	161.44	1280.52	1462.06	111.98	—	1395.00	932.65
HYV Wheat	209.60	244.80	844.80	714.72	—	74.26	381.60	224.40
Pulses	117.60	122.40	323.88	380.60	—	62.75	462.20	284.80
Oil seeds	57.60	52.80	476.36	493.011	—	—	336.80	333.60

SOURCE: GKP, FMS Report, 1979-80.

[28] In the absence of data on land transfers, it is difficult to comment on the nature of land alienation in Kusthtia.

TABLE 4.8: DISTRIBUTION OF LAND AND FARM ACCORDING TO
DIFFERENT SIZE GROUPS GKP, 1981-2

Farm Size Group	No. of Farms Involved	Percentage of Farm in the Group	Percentage of Total Farm in the Group
Less than 2.00 acres	283	38.14	7.44
2.00 to 3.99 acres	206	27.76	27.12
4.00 to 5.99 acres	123	16.58	19.36
6.00 to 7.99 acres	57	7.68	13.35
8.00 to 9.99 acres	29	3.91	8.33
10.00 and above	44	5.93	24.40
Total	742	100.00	100.00

SOURCE: BWDB Report, Kushtia Unit I.

tendency towards land consolidation by the rich farmers. The FMSR data do not give us any idea about the changes in the tenancy system in the GKP command area. Arens and Beurden (1977) who carried out fieldwork in Kushtia noted a decline in the tenancy arrangement in the irrigated areas. They noted a steady rise in the number of rural proletariat largely due to the evictions of tenants. The FMSR data neither give information on the tenancy arrangement nor on the wage labour. Anyhow the problem may be examined with the help of village-level data.

In the absence of FMSR data on the extent of tenancy and landlessness in the GKP command area, not much can be said about the impact of the technological changes on the rural poor. However, there remains little doubt about the fact that tenurial insecurity, unfavourable terms and conditions for the tenants land alienation will have an adverse effect on the economic condition of the rural poor. Very little changes in the wage rate, demographic pressures on the labour market and lack of employment opportunities have worsened the living conditions of the rural poor.

4.4 A CASE STUDY

The village Naopara is located on the western side of Kushtia district under the jurisdiction of Mirpur Upazilla. Oral evidence of the residents of Naopara suggests that the village is more than three hundred years old. It figured in the Rennels Map in 1770. The first survey of the village took place in 1855 as a part of Thak survey all over Bengal. However, the first detailed account of the landholding structure of the village can be found in the Cadestral Survey report. During this survey a map was prepared to show the cropping plots, roads, rivers, etc.[29] During the mid-sixties, the Pakistan Government carried out a *mouza*-wise survey to assess the changes in the landholding structure.[30] The quality of this survey data appeared to be extremely poor as most of the records were compiled on a reporting basis. A tendency for over-reporting was common as many land-owners staked claim on lands deserted by the Hindu *zamindars*. As compared to the village in Nadia district, official reports about Naopara during the post-Partition period is extremely sketchy.[31]

A better communication network helped Mirpur region as well as the village to keep in touch with the outside world right from the early part of this century. A railway track connected Mirpur with the commercial centres like Kushtia town, Ranaghat, Krishna Nagar, Santipur and Calcutta (see Map 6). Navigation through the river Garai and its tributaries helped the movement of commercial goods from Mirpur to other areas. After Partition, a highway connected Mirpur and the village with Kushtia, Meherpur, Gangni, Bheramera and a number of small and medium-sized commercial centres. Transportation of goods through rail, road and rivers helped the process of commercialization of agriculture in the entire area.

The Partition in 1947 brought about a large number of changes in agriculture in Mirpur. The region lost its important markets for commercial goods in West Bengal. The two newly independent states severed links of railways, roads and rivers. The Partition uprooted the Hindu peasants in the area. It took time for the new settlers from West Bengal to settle their claims and to begin cultivation again. The land policy of the Pakistan Government was not clear enough. All it did was to abolish the *zamindari* system through the State Acquisition Act and impose a ceiling of 100 *bighas* per family. The ceiling was raised from 100 to 300 *bighas* in 1961. Inconsistencies in land policies created further problem for the peasantry. Like other areas in East Bengal, Mirpur and its environs went through a period of crisis and uncertainty following Partition.

[29] Some aspects of CS report have been discussed in Chapter Two.

[30] This was known as State Acquisition Survey (SAS).

[31] The Bangladesh Government carried out Revenue Survey during the mid-eighties through plot to plot enumerations. The survey included information from each village about the land-owners, the size of holding, revenue paid, etc. A map of each *mouza* was also prepared. The survey was nearing completion in Kushtia in 1989.

NAOPARA C. S. MAUZA

N

NAOPARA   PURAN
MAUZA

KRISHNAPUR

CHUNIAPARA   MAUZA

Mora Garai River

Map 11. Naopara Cadestral Survey Map.

In 1989, the village Naopara had 209 households of which 204 belonged to the Muslims and 5 to the Hindus. It had a total population of 1198, 1165 Muslims and 33 Hindus. The village is located by the side of the Kushtia-Meherpur main road. Most of the houses are situated close to the road. The vast area in the north and north-eastern part of the village is used for agricultural purposes. The GK canal flows through the centre of the village. The river Mora Garai bifurcates the village on the south-western part (see Map 11). Except during the monsoon, the river remains dry throughout the year. It is a tributary of the Garai river which flows through Kushtia town. The village is surrounded by densely populated *mouzas* like Chuniapara, Jogipara, Naoparapuran and Krishnapur.

In 1989, out of a total of 385.45 acres of land, 256.08 acres were suitable for cultivation. The GK canal provides water to about two-third of cultivable land. The main road and homesteads cover an area of 41.84 acres and the canal takes as much as 50.26 acres (Table 4.9). The spread of irrigation which ensured water supply during the *kharif* I and II seasons has helped double cropping in almost the entire cultivable land, either *aman* and jute, or *aus* and another vegetable. A number of new crops are now grown in the village. The cultivation of tobacco, oil seeds and a number of vegetables like cauliflower, brinjal, tomato and cucumber had become popular among the farmers. Today the cultivable land in the village is used more intensively for agricultural production.

The GK canal offered the much needed security to the farmers of Naopara by ensuring supply of water during the two *kharif* seasons. The GKP with its extension work played a catalytic role in spreading HYVs,

TABLE 4.9: CLASSIFICATION OF LAND OF NAOPARA, 1989

Type of Land	Area (in acres)	Percentage
Homestead (including road and marketplace)	41.84	11
Cultivable	256.08	66
GK Canal	50.26	13
Tank	14.24	4
Bamboo grove	9.88	3
Others	13.15	3
Total	385.45	100

fertilizers and pesticides. The use of modern inputs increased the cost of production of most of the crops. However, the rise in the yield rate helped the farmers to earn profit. In order to understand the nature of profit from the cultivation of HYVs, let us consider the cost of production of two major crops. The cost of production of HYV crops vary according to the use of ploughing, seeds, fertilizers, pesticides and labour. For example, the average cost of production of *aus* in a bigha of land is 1455 TK and the average yield rate of *aus* from a *bigha* of land is around 10 *maunds*.[32] In 1988-9, the market price of a *maund* of *aus* was 225 TK. Therefore, on simple calculations, after deducting all essential expenses on production a farmer could earn a profit of 795 TK by cultivating HYV *aus*. In the case of *aman*, both the yield rate as well as profit is higher than *aus*.[33] On an average, a farmer gets 18 *maunds* of

TABLE 4.10: PRIMARY AGRICULTURAL OCCUPATIONS AND
CLASS POSITION OF VILLAGE HOUSEHOLDS, NAOPARA, 1989

Primary Agricultural	Class	Number	Percentage
Land-owner (over 5 acres)	I	14	7
Land-owner (between 1 and 5 acres)	II	22	10
Land-owner-Sharecropper (owned and leased in land less than 1 acre)	II	10	5
Land-owner-Sharecropper (owned and leased in land less than 1 acre)	III	12	6
Sharecropper	III	10	5
Landless Labourer	III	101	48
Labourer-Sharecropper	III	10	5
Labourer-Landowner	III	24	11
Non-agricultural Occupations	—	6	3
Total		209	100

[32] Cost of production for *aus* in a *bigha* of land may be calculated by adding cost on ploughing (230 TK), seeds (65 TK), fertilizers (210 TK), pesticides (70 TK) and labour (880 TK).

[33] Calculated by adding ploughing (230 TK), seeds (65 TK), fertilizers (210 TK), pesticides (70 TK), labour (780 TK).

aman from a bigha of land. In 1988-9, the price of *aman* in the open market was 280 TK. Thus, in the case of *aman* too, a farmer was in a position to have a profit of 3685 TK. The higher yield rate and better price for most of the agricultural produce have encouraged the farmers to adopt new techniques of production. The advent of irrigation has brightened the prospect of profit in the village.

Unlike Bira, land distribution in Naopara has remained skewed for many years. As a result, the beneficiaries of new technologies are mostly the rich farmers. By taking into account primary occupations of each household and the extent of land-ownership, a three-tier class structure can be drawn. First, those who belong to class I are rich farmers, each family owning more than five acres of land and using either sharecroppers or landless labourers for cultivation. As many as fifteen households belong to this category and own 45 per cent of cultivable land. Second, class II comprising land-owners owning between one and five acres and land-owners-cum-sharecroppers owing and leasing in more than one acre. Altogether twenty-five households belong to this class and control twenty seven per cent cultivable land. Third, most of the households owning less than an acre have mixed occupations, e.g. land-owner-cum-sharecropper, land-owner-cum-labourer, sharecropper-cum-labourer and landless labourers constitute class III. A total of a hundred and fifty-two households comprise class III (Tables 4.10 and 4.11).[34] In the vernacular, farmers in class I are called *dhani krishak* and those in class II are known as *grihasta* or self-sufficient peasants. Various local terms are used for those in class III, e.g. *garib chasi, jon majur, bhag chasi* and the like. It will have to be emphasized that primary occupations and extent of land-ownership do not give us an entirely satisfactory picture of agrarian hierarchy as certain amount of heterogeneity can be noticed within a class. For example, land-owners-cum-labourers in class III may be

[34] Many writers have commented on the nature of agrarian hierarchy in Bangladesh. van Schendel (1972), for example, divided the rural population into four categories by an ascending alphabetical order of A, B, C and D where A implied the lowest and D the highest socio-economic category. For van Schendel, the standard of living and economic conditions are more important in categorizing a peasant household than the ownership of land. Westergaard (1986) classified rural population into landless, marginal, small subsistence, medium subsistence and surplus peasants. See also Chowdhury (1978), Jahangir (1979), Rehman (1986) and Wood (1976).

TABLE 4.11: LANDHOLDING SIZE AND AREA UNDER SIZE-CLASS
IN NAOPARA, 1989

Size	Land (in acres)	Percentage
.00-.50	28.70	12
.51-1.00	29.54	12
1.01-1.50	20.02	8
1.51-2.00	13.06	6
2.01-3.00	10.03	4
3.01-4.00	22.71	9
4.01-5.00	24.00	10
5.01 and above	98.02	39
Total	246.08	100

differentiated on the basis of extent of land-ownership. Out of nineteen
households, six own less than .10 acres, five household own between
11 and .30 acres and the rest own between .31and .99 acres. Moreover,
demographic size of each household, income from non-agricultural
sources and ownership of livestock animals can also influence the
hierarchical structure. However, two necessary but not sufficient
determining factors of agrarian hierarchy in the context of Bangladesh
are land-ownership and primary occupation (see Map 12).

The extent of land ownership of those in class I and II has risen in
Naopara in recent years as a result of land alienation. The data on land
transfer would give us an idea about the nature of land sales in Naopara.
Land transfer data available at the Land Registry Office (LRO) in Mirpur
shows trends in land sales and purchases.[35] In 1988-9, the LRO recorded
33 cases of land transfers in the village amounting to 20.04 acres of land.
The data shows a trend in the transfer of land from the hands of farmers
belonging to class III to those in class I. The rising cost of production
of HYV crops, various kinds of contingencies, e.g. medical expenses,
death and marriage account for the rise in land alienation. The spread
of irrigation and higher yield rate and profit from crops like paddy,

[35] The LRO data do not include all kinds of land transfers within the
village. For example, land transfers due to usufructuary mortagage are not
recorded. In order to avoid expenses on registration, many transactions take
place without an intimation to LRO.

NAOPARA R.S. MAUZA 1989

KRISHNAPUR

NAOPARA PURAN
MAUZA

G. K. CANAL

CHUNIA PARA

Mora Garai River

Map 12. Naopara Today.

vegetables, jute and tobacco encourage rich farmers to buy and reinvest more on land. For example, 41-year-old Nazmal Karim owned 15 acres of irrigated and 6.75 acres of unirrigated land in 1989. Besides producing *aman* and *aus*, Nazmal grows tobacco, a commercial crop in about 8 acres as the rate of profit is higher in the case of tobacco cultivation. In a *bigha* of land, tobacco cultivation costs him approximately 2600 TK, for ploughing, seeds, fertilizers, pesticides and labour. The average yield rate of tobacco in a *bigha* varies between 30 and 35 *maunds*. In 1989, the market rate of a *maund* of tobacco was 1600 TK. Thus, from simple calculation the profit can go up to 40,000 TK from the cultivation of tobacco in a *bigha* of land. Bangladesh Leaf Tobacco Company in Kushtia offers incentives to farmers, e.g. loans, firewood for the preparation of leaves and even transportation costs for carrying the crop from the field to the factory. The tobacco cultivation has become popular in the village due to the fact that, unlike other non-cereal crops like jute or sugarcane, the sale price of tobacco has remained steady throughout the eighties. With the support of tobacco companies, rich farmers of Naopara like Nazmul Karim now invest more on tobacco. This also means a shift in the mode of cultivation, from tenancy to hired labour, as incentive from tobacco companies are offered to land-owners who cultivate either with the help of household labour or by hiring wage labourers. Moreover, splitting up of sizeable profit with the sharecroppers is also not an attractive proposition from the point of view of the land-owners. The growth of a commercial crop like tobacco has made investment on land a more lucrative proposition and encouraged land consolidation by the rich farmers in the village.

Sharecroppers in Naopara have very little to gain from the spread of new technologies. In Bangladesh, land-owners make oral contracts before leasing out land and when a sharecropper fails to satisfy the owner in raising yield rate or in using better inputs, he faces the inevitable consequences of eviction. Most oral contracts are made for a year, although leasing out land for only one crop is also common. Some land-owners use hired labour in a plot of land for one crop and lease out the same plot to a sharecropper for the second crop. In general, sharecroppers in Naopara receive 50 per cent crop and bear all essential expenses for production except land revenue and irrigation charges. Expenditure on seeds, manure, fertilizers, pesticides, labour, ploughing, transplantation, etc., and bullock hiring charges are borne entirely by the sharecroppers. Expenses at the time of harvesting, e.g. crop cutting, winnowing and transporting, are met by the land-owners and sharecroppers separately as the division of produce takes place right on the field when the crop is ready for harvesting. However, in the case of some crops like jute and vegetables land-owners prefer to take the rent in cash. In such cases, the sharecroppers pay 50 per cent of cash earnings to the land-owners.

There are two factors which are particularly important in influencing land-owners decision to lease out land. Firstly, location of land in the far off areas compel many land-owners to use sharecroppers. For example, Haji Samsul Haq, a land-owner of 70 bighas, leased out 16 bighas as the land was located outside Naopara. Similarly, Mojammel Haq, a land-owner of a neighbouring village who owned 3 acres of land in Naopara leased them out to the sharecroppers in the village. Land-owners who are residing in Kushtia town or Mirpur prefer to do the same. Secondly, sharecropping arrangements suit those who are engaged in non agricultural white collar jobs in the village or nearby towns. In these cases fixed rent in cash simplifies the problems of rent collection. Land-owning households with a single female member, widow, aged or disabled in most cases have very little option but to rely on the sharecroppers. Thus, land-owners lease out land more out of compulsion than choice.

Disputes between land-owners and sharecroppers are common, so are the evictions. As mentioned earlier, land-owners' dissatisfaction with the yield is a common point of dispute. Sharecroppers are often rebuked for not using adequate HYVs, fertilizers and manure. The termination cases of sharecropping contracts in recent years show that they take place as a result of land-owners' complaint of negligence on the part of the sharecroppers and their inability to produce enough. However, from the point of view of the sharecroppers, the terminations of contract or evictions have become a regular phenomenon especially after the inception of canal water irrigation in the village. A sharecropper who is in a better position to invest more on HYVs, fertilizers and pesticides stands a good chance of securing a lease for the second time.

Besides lack of tenurial security, the burden of debt and rising costs of inputs have acted as barrier to the spread of new technologies among the sharecroppers. For example, Shamsuddin, a 37-year-old sharecropper, leased in 6 *bighas* of irrigated land for a year. In order to meet higher cost of inputs, he borrowed 3,000 TK from a land-owner cum-moneylender for a period of 5 months with 50 per cent rate of interest. After meeting expenses on seeds, manure, fertilizers, pesticides, labour, bullocks, etc., and after paying 50 per cent crop to the land-owner, Shamsuddin's received a meagre share for himself. Therefore, inadequate resources and a high rate of interest on loans worked as constraining factors in the diffusion of new technologies. Land-owners-cum-sharecroppers leasing in more than an acre too face similar problems.

Therefore, compared to West Bengal, sharecroppers in Bangladesh villages are now at the receiving end. In Bira, as we noticed earlier, sharecroppers played the role of enterprising farmers and were instrumental in popularizing modern inputs. The state protected the interests of the sharecroppers and the process of mobilization helped them to assert their rights. However, in Bangladesh, the absence of a programme of the state for protecting tenurial rights of the sharecroppers and the non-existence of peasant associations have worsened their condition. This has resulted in inefficient agricultural production under-leased in land.

The agricultural labourers in Naopara are of different types. For example, there are free wage labourers locally known as *jon majur*, who work on a daily wage basis and receive wages in cash and kind. The *jon majurs* are indispensable for agricultural works like ploughing, sowing, weeding and transplanting and for the use of fertilizers and pesticides. They enjoy the freedom to choose their employers and receive a daily wage of 25 *Taka* and a midday meal for 8 hours of work. However, the numerically strongest in the village are *khola majur*, who work under a land-owner as a team for one crop or for a year.[36] During the spare time, *khola* labourers are free to work under other employers. In many ways *khola* labour arrangement resembles *thika* labour in the Indian countryside. In both cases, labourers are paid a fixed wage for a specified job and are free to determine a time limit for the completion of the job. However, *khola* labourers always work as a group, comprising 4 to 6 members. Besides these labourers, there are attached, or *badha majurs*, mostly young boys between the age group 10 and 20 who live in the land-owner's house and receive yearly payment in cash (ranging

---

[36] This is similar to what van Schendel and Faraizi (1984) described as seasonal labour. These labourers pledge labour for a stipulated period against a fixed remuneration and during that period they are exclusively bound to the employer. They offer services during the peak periods like transplanting and harvesting. The attraction for this kind of labour is that the labourer earns high wages for two to four months and retains the freedom to seek employment elsewhere for the rest of the year.

between 300 to 400 *Taka* in a year), with meals and clothes. The wage rate depends on the age and physical ability of the labourer. *Badha* labourers can be used both for farm and off-farm work, e.g. ploughing, weeding, harvesting, looking after livestock, cleaning the household, etc. This labour arrangement suits many land-owners as these labourers can be employed throughout the year to perform various kinds of household and agricultural work.

The use of new technologies have influenced the employment opportunities in the village. Irrigation, HYVs and fertilizers have raised the demand for labour. During the HYV *aus* crop cultivation, an agricultural labourer gets work in the field for about 28 days in the months of *Baisakh* (April-May) and *Jyestha* (May-June) for ploughing, sowing and transplanting, 10 days in *Asar* (June-July) for weeding and 30 days each in *Shravan* (July-August), *Bhadra* (August-September), for harvesting as well as for ploughing and transplanting of *aman* crop. In *Ashvin* (September-October), a labour gets 10 days work for weeding field under *aman* crop and in *Kartik* (October-November) work for about 5 days is available for spraying pesticides. The whole of *Agrahan* (November-December) is used for harvesting *aman* crop. The development of irrigation facilities succeeded in providing some additional work in the lean months like *Paus* (December-January), *Magh* (January-February) and *Phalgun* (February-March). The demand for labourers for the traditional crops in non-irrigated area is far less than for HYV crops in irrigated area. However, the rise in the demand for labourers has not made an impact on the wage rate. Even after the introduction of new technologies, wage rates fluctuate in accordance with the demand for labourers. In other words, agricultural workers have not been successful in receiving a fixed wage throughout the year. Nor have they been successful in fetching the stipulated wage fixed by the Government of Bangladesh.[37] During the peak period a labourer may receive between 20 and 25 *Taka* and a midday meal. The wage may drop to 15 *Taka* a day and a midday meal in the lean period. On an average, a *khola* labourer manages to get between 30 and 35 *Taka* a day. The traditional practice of payment of wage in kind at the time of harvesting is still common in Naopara. For harvesting 8 *maunds* of paddy, a labourer can

---

[37] The minimum daily wage for agricultural labourers was fixed at 3.5 *seers* of rice or its equivalent in cash in the Bangladesh Land Reforms Ordinance, 1984.

receive one and half *maund*. For harvesting 80 *kathas* or 4 *bighas* of land a labourer gets crops grown in 14 *kathas* or little more than half a *bigha*. The measurement of crop in a basket for the payment of wage is also common. A basketful of paddy weighs about 5 kg. In the case of *aman* paddy, a labourer gets 18 baskets of paddy for every 80 baskets taken by the land-owner. In the case of *aus*, a labourer receives 14 baskets for every 80 baskets for the owner.[38] Harvesting is often done by the *khola* labourers and crops received as wage are equally divided among the members of the group.

It is believed that in agriculturally advanced areas in Bangladesh where wages are paid in cash, especially after the harvest, the labourers get more. However, Rahman (1984) rightly points out that in the peak seasons in the late seventies agricultural labourers in some agriculturally advanced areas received a wage of 12.46 TK a day. But real wage at the 1973-4 cost of living was only 6.79 TK. This has been the overall trend in the country since the late seventies.

Although the spread of new technologies has improved employment opportunities in the village, corresponding changes in the real wage rate have not come about. This is also the case at the national level. Khan (1984) who examined the changes in the real wage rates throughout the seventies noted that real wages hardly increased; at times they droped. Khan converted money wage into real wage by taking into account cost of living as well as equivalent coarse rice.[39] His data pertaining to 1973-4 to 1979-80 period show negligible changes in the real wage rate, it declined in 1973-4, 1977-8 and 1979-80 (Table 4.12). The conversion of money wage rate into kilograms of coarse rice in the village in 1987-8 and 1988-9 too dropped from 3 to 2.75 kg, although the increase in money wage during the same period was 15 to 20 TK.[40] The rate of payment of wage in kind to labourers during the post-harvest period had remained the same during the 1987-8 and 1988-9 period. In terms of real wage, the payment in kind, which has not declined, would be more desirable from the point of view of the labourers. However, land-owners pay in kind only during the post-harvest period in order to

[38] The measurement in basket is more common than other forms of payment of wage to a labourer at the end of the harvest of the crop.

[39] Khan (1984: 85-9).

[40] Such conversions into rice to determine real wage has been done in other case studies. van Schendel (1982).

TABLE 4.12: AGRICULTURAL WAGES IN BANGLADESH
BETWEEN 1973-4 AND 1979-80

Year	Money Wage (TK/Person/ per day)	Real Wage (TK/Person/ day at 1973-4 Cost of living)	Wage Rate in kg of Coarse Rice
1973-4	6.69	6.69	2.36
1974-5	9.05	5.33	1.57
1975-6	8.82	7.09	2.61
1976-7	8.93	7.32	2.96
1977-8	9.44	6.41	2.43
1978-9	10.88	7.28	2.53
1979-80	12.46	6.79	2.16

SOURCE: Khan (1984).

meet labour shortage in the peak time.[41] An increase in the man-land ratio and migration of labourers from other areas depress the wage rate in the village.[42]

The labourers enjoy little bargaining power in the fixation of minimum wage. For example, in June 1989, at the time of transplantation of *aman*, the daily wage rate for the agricultural labourers was 25 TK. However, one of the land-owners managed to hire labourers from neighbouring villages at the rate of 20 TK. This led to an altercation between the land-owner and labourers. The matter was referred to the Salishi Board (dispute settlement board) consisting of the elderly members of the village for an amicable settlement. The Board observed that the land-owners had freedom to hire labourers from outside. Such disputes over wages are quite common in Naopara in recent times. However, in the absence of organized protests, the land-owners do not find it hard to get away with their plans. Labour hiring methods too act as

[41] Rahman (1984: 12-14) noted that in areas where labourers received wage in cash during the peak seasons, they lost a great deal. For example, in 1973-4 in some agriculturally advanced districts, labourers received 12.46 TK as daily wage. At 1973-4 cost of living, the real wage was only 6.79 TK.
[42] In the context of declining real wage rate in the country as a whole, Khan (1984: 191) argued that slow growth of employment in non-agricultural sector, worsening land-man and land-labour ratio and demographic pressures account for this kind of situation.

constraining factor in the bargaining process. Some land-owners prefer the *khola* labour arrangement in order to ensure supply of labour during the peak periods. As most of these *khola* labour contracts take place much before the actual agricultural operations, labourers get very little chance to bargain over wages or to make new demands. Land-owners often offer loans to agricultural labourers to bind them under obligation to work. When a daily wage labourer gets trapped into such borrowing, he is obliged to work in the land of the moneylender and receive only two-third of the actual wage; the rest is deducted as interest for the loan. *Khola* labourers also borrow during the lean periods and repay after the harvest. When a *khola* labourer borrows a *maund* of paddy in the lean months, he returns one *maund* and twenty *seers* after the harvest. This kind of lending arrangement not only binds the labourers under obligation to work under the lender-cum-land-owner and to remain subdued but also compels them to pay a high rate of interest.[43] Therefore, though new technologies have increased employment opportunities for the labourers in Naopara, drop in the real wage, traditional modes of payment of wage and debt traps have worsened their conditions over the years.

State programmes, e.g. surplus land redistribution among the agricultural labourers, conferment of rights on homestead land and employment generation programme like 'food for work', have not yet been carried out in most Bangladeshi villages. Some of the important components of land reforms package are simply missing. Neither peasant associations nor local-level political bodies like *panchayats* have come up to protect the interests of the poor.[44] The state, in order to maintain status quo, is following policies to protect the rural rich. Agricultural taxation policies, principles for distribution of inputs like HYVs, fertilizers and public works programme have not bridged the gap between the rich and the poor in the context of Bangladesh.[45]

The only silver lining in this kind of scenario is the emergence of a

[43] Pure cash loans without any preconditions involve a higher rate of interest. For borrowing 100 TK, a labourer pays 150 TK after a gap of three months, in which case the rate of interest goes up to 200 per cent.

[44] Left parties have not been successful in reaching out to the rural poor. Two other national parties, the Awami League and the Bangladesh Nationalist Party (BNP) have no peasant associations in Kushtia.

[45] Rahman (1986: 12-14) noted various attempts by the state to protect the interest of the landowning class and in maintaining *status quo*.

number of NGOs and *gram sarkars* (GSs) in Bangladesh to take up the cause of the rural poor in some areas. Elections for GSs were held in 1980 to build a village-level power structure for the implementation of developmental programmes. So far the Union Parishads functioned as the only lower-level organization with a population of about 20,000. But GSs were created to cover a maximum 5,000 people. In Kushtia, several small villages were combined to form one GSs. In cases where several small villages formed one GS, the smallest units gained very little. This was the case with Naopara too. Being the smallest constituent unit of the GS, Naopara was unable to use it to its advantage. Moreover, initial enthusiasms with the GS fizzled out with the military takeover of power in 1982.

The NGOs have been active in mobilizing the rural poor in some parts of Bangladesh.[46] NGOs like SETU, The Bangladesh Rural Advancement Committee (BRAC), Gono Sastho Kendra (GSK) and Nijera Kori have branches in Kushtia too.[47] The BRAC was formed in the early seventies to assist in the resettlement of refugees in the aftermath of the liberation war. Its target people are those who do not own any productive assets and survive by selling physical labour. Nijera Kori formed Bangladesh Bhumihin Samiti (Bangladesh Land-less Labourers' Association) in some areas to protect the interests of the labourers. The Grameen Bank branches offered loans to landless labourers and small farmers at a nominal rate of interest.[48] All these NGOs have potential to offer much needed support to the poor in rural areas. However, in 1989 except SETU none of these NGOs had organizations in Naopara. SETU was primarily concerned with the problems of women's education, health care, handicrafts and forestry. Nowadays, though SETU is not directly involved in organizing rural labourers or sharecroppers, it serves an important function of raising consciousness among the poor about their objective conditions of living. The raising of consciousness in the long run will

[46] According to Hassan (1985), there were about 200 NGOs operating in Bangladesh in the mid-eighties.

[47] GSK was initially organized as a field hospital for Mukti Bahini during the liberation war in 1971. Later it provided primary health care services. It also played a crucial role in formulating drug polices of the Government of Bangladesh.

[48] It has now become a part of the government banking system with 632 branches all over Bangladesh and total investment of 5.7 billion *Takas*.

surely have an effect on the relation of domination and subordination in rural Bangladesh.[49] The NGOs through their consciousness raising programme have created an ideal condition for the mobilization of the rural poor and protection of their rights.

---

[49] As Freire (1972) notes in his theory of conscientization.

CHAPTER FIVE

Conclusion

The new technology has spread at a rapid rate in some areas in Bengal in recent times. The spread is particularly successful in those districts where surface and under-surface water have been tapped for irrigation purposes. Agrarian changes in Nadia and Kushtia have come about largely due to the development of irrigation infrastructure. Irrigation has played a similar role in agricultural development in many other parts of Asia. Ishikawa (1974) rightly described it as the 'leading input' in agricultural modernization.[1] An extensive use of HYVs, fertilizers and pesticides in areas where irrigation intensity is high indicates complementary nature of use of major inputs for agricultural growth. This has been the case in most green revolution belts in West Bengal and Bangladesh.

Literature on the spread of new technology in Indian agriculture is replete with examples of its adverse effects on the rural poor. Many writers have commented on the development of skewed land holding pattern in agriculturally advanced areas, some have shown deteriorating terms and conditions in tenurial contract and evictions of unregistered tenants. The rise in the number of 'rural proletariats' featured prominently in some of the writing on the new technology in agriculture. As far as Bengal is concerned, the impact of technological

[1] He identifies four successive stages in land productivity in Asian agriculture. In the first stage, land productivity remains very low and irrigation becomes a 'leading input', in the second phase, it helps to stabilize harvest fluctuations arising from variable rainfall. It allows the introduction of a second crop. In the third stage too, irrigation acts as a leading input and makes possible an increased use of HYVs, fertilizers. In the fourth and final stage, other complementary inputs, fertilizers, seeds and improved techniques become the 'combined leading input'. The correlation of irrigation level with land productivity now declines, while the correlation of fertilizer intensity with land productivity becomes more important (1967: 90-2).

change on agrarian communities is one of a mixed kind. The spread of new technology has not aggravated the rural inequities in West Bengal the way it has done so in the neighbouring state of Bangladesh. Some of the factors which helped in improving conditions in West Bengal have been discussed at length in this study. Factors accounting for deterioration in Bangladesh agriculture too have been examined.

The genesis of agricultural backwardness can be traced back to the colonial period. The growth of cash crop cultivation like jute, sugarcane brought the local commodity market closer to the global economy. Fluctuations in the price of cash crop in the international market had disastrous effect on the peasantry in Bengal. During the two world wars and great depressions in the thirties when the prices of agricultural produce, especially cash crops, reached an all-time low, the peasantry in Bengal faced starvation as they were unable to withstand risk and uncertainty.[2] This was also the time when the traders-cum-money-lenders tightened their grip over the peasantry of Bengal. Like other parts of Bengal, in Nadia too the development of cash crop cultivation and its linkage with the outside market had cast their spell on the peasantry.

From the early part of the present century some perceptible gains in agriculture came about in Bengal as a result of land reclamation and increase in cropping intensity. However, a steady rate of growth of population right from 1901-11 led to an unfavourable land-man ratio and marginalized the gains from agricultural production. The percentage variation of population was particularly high in the Presidency division (including Nadia) as between 1931 and 1941 it went up to 26.80. Studies on the population structure in Bengal during the late colonial period show migration as a more important factor in influencing demographic composition than changes in fertility and mortality. The impact of human migration on agrarian structure in Nadia during the late colonial period and at the time of Partition had been phenomenal.

When the colonial rule came to an end, the prospect for agricultural growth in the two halves of Bengal looked extremely bleak. The land reclamation process reached a saturation point, further increase in the yield rate was also not feasible for lack of irrigation and other inputs. The political instability in the regions and Partition which uprooted

[2] Bose (1986), Chaudhuri (1983). Greenough (1982) examined in detail the various implications of this trend in Bengal agriculture.

millions of peasants created further problems in the agricultural sector of newly independent states. Both West Bengal and the then East Pakistan faced the gigantic task of rehabilitating uprooted peasants. Very little resources were available for initiating new programmes for agricultural growth. Thus, Bengal agriculture was passing through one of its worst crises. However, it did not take too long for newly independent states to initiate programmes for agrarian reforms. Land reform acts were adopted in the mid-fifties in West Bengal in order to abolish the *zamindari* land tenure arrangement. Ceilings on land holdings were imposed, attempts were made to protect tenurial rights and programmes were undertaken to redistribute surplus lands among the poor peasants. However, all these measures did not bring the desired results. Land ceiling provisions were evaded, tenants were evicted and various unscrupulous methods were discovered to stall the land redistribution programme. These developments prompted hard thinking on land reforms. The popular mandate to the United Front in 1967 cleared the deck for actions on agrarian matters. The tenure of the United Front was too short to implement its reform programmes. However, the initiatives of the United Front helped to create a new awareness in rural West Bengal. A movement to grab *benami* land of the *jotedars* swept through parts of the state. The UF government formulated its programme on the kisan front. The CPI(M) leader spelt about its party programme in the following way:

Our party should ceaselessly educate the peasants and agricultural labourers that the basic slogan of abolition of landlordism without compensation and giving of land to the agricultural labourers and poor peasants free of cost is to be realized through the mass action of entire peasantry... It is possible for strong, militant and well-organized movements of poor peasants and agricultural labourers to force the unwilling governments and landlords to distribute fallow lands to some extent. It is also possible, through effective mass struggles, to prevent the eviction of tenants from the lands that they are cultivating and to achieve land for house-sites for the rural poor free of cost, to a limited extent. (1976: 7)[3]

However, the political instability in the state and the Congress rule since 1972 did not help much to carry forward the land reforms programme initiated by the United Front, especially its attempts to confiscate surplus lands and to protect the interests of sharecroppers

---

[3] Konar (1977), see Mitter (1977).

and agricultural labourers. There was a lull in the land reforms programme in West Bengal between 1972 and 1977.

Agrarian reforms received utmost priority when the Left Front came into office in 1977. Several amendments to land reforms acts were proposed and a special drive was launched to register the names of sharecroppers. Data on the use of irrigation and modern inputs show an upward trend since the late seventies. Food production data too show a rise in the production of almost all major crops. The rise in the production of *boro* was particularly phenomenal. The present study on the nature of use of the new technology and changes in food production in Nadia district confirm this trend. Data pertaining to agrarian change in Nadia and in one of its villages show some new developments. Sharecroppers now enjoy tenurial rights, receive stipulated share of agricultural produce and play an active role in agricultural production. Small cultivators too are beneficiaries of the technological change in agriculture as they have gained access to irrigation and other inputs. Agricultural labourers have benefited due to an increase in man days and real wage.

Some broad similarities in the agricultural development programme in West Bengal and Bangladesh can easily be discerned. First of all, like West Bengal in Bangladesh too, several measures were adopted to abolish landlordism and to introduce new technologies to augment agricultural production. Bangladesh too achieved success in spreading modern inputs including irrigation in some of its districts. Food production rose in these districts in the eighties. However, land alienation, especially from the hands of small cultivators to rich farmers, is on the rise in green revolution belts and eviction of tenants has become rampant. Terms of sharecropping contract weigh heavily in favour of land-owners.[4] A drop in the real wage has worsened the condition of the wage labourers. Programmes like redistribution of surplus lands among the labourers, fixation of minimum wage rate and food-for-work have not made any headway in Bangladesh. Moreover, migration of labourers from agriculturally backward regions to green revolution belt has created further problems. Even after agrarian reforms, land-power nexus has remained unaffected.

Bharadwaj (1974) did see the possibility of the emergence of the rich peasantry in the green revolution belts. She noted, the new technology

---

[4] This is similar to the trends as noticed by many observers in the green revolution belts of India in the late sixties, e.g. Bardhan (1970), Frankel (1971).

based on the improved seeds, new techniques, adequate supply of irrigation, etc., even if they are scale neutral, might benefit the bigger farmers to a greater extent. The rich farmers may be in a better position to exploit new opportunities with their relatively easier access to credit. The pattern of land lease might alter as investment becomes a profitable enterprise. According to Bharadwaj, 'Large owners may gradually shift towards capitalist farming relying on the use of hired labour. Thus if the green revolution persists and spreads, it may lead to significant qualitative (not only quantitative) changes in the village economy' (1974: 10). Moreover, a moneylender-cum-merchant may extract a very high rate of interest by giving commodity loans. Such interlocking of markets increases the exploitative power of the land-owner.

In the context of agricultural growth in West Bengal it was pointed out that the state intervention, adoption of policies like 'operation barga' have adversely affected the rich peasantry. However, it was different as far as agrarian changes in Bangladesh are concerned. Some aspects of the dominance of the landowning class in controlling markets, tenancy arrangements and wage labour were mentioned earlier. These developments are similar to those described by Bharadwaj.

The differential impact of technological growth on the agrarian communities in Bengal can be explained by referring to two crucial factors. First, state intervention in development programme in West Bengal has had a number of positive effects. For example, conferment of tenurial rights to sharecroppers, fixation of minimum wage for agricultural labourers, enforcement of land ceiling programme and redistribution of surplus lands came about as a result of state intervention.[5] A major part of state resources was spent on developing irrigation programmes and subsidizing inputs. State programmes like OB and *panchayati* system have succeeded in breaking land-power nexus and alleviating rural poverty.

The supporting role of the state, as one notices in the case of West Bengal is non-existent in Bangladesh. One cannot agree more with Rahman (1986) when he writes that the state in Bangladesh is, in complete control of nation's economy and bureaucracy is the *de facto* owner and manager of the system. A close review of land reforms and various other programmes in Bangladesh brings out the partisan character of the state. Appeasement of the rural rich through its input distribution programme or credit disbursment policies is evident.

[5] Joshi (1975: 88) describes them as 'land reforms from above'.

van Schendel (1981) notes that the process of democratization in Bangladesh in the late eighties has strengthened the position of the rural elite in the function of the state. The repressive nature of state policies came into open when popular protests were throttled in the late eighties.

The second factor in influencing growth and equity in West Bengal and Bangladesh is the changes in relations of power. *Panchayat* elections on the basis of universal adult franchise and party political affiliation were held in West Bengal to raise an awareness among the rural masses and to decentralize economic power. *Panchayat* elections offered an opportunity to poorer section to take part in local-level power structure and in the decision-making process.[6] A number of developmental programmes are now being implemented and monitored with the help of the *panchayats*. *Panchayats* were instrumental in 'operation barga' programme. The changes in the local power structure have also weakened the traditional dependency relations between the rural rich and the poor. However, in Bangladesh, no attempt has yet been made to develop local-level bodies to give representation to the underprivileged. Experiments were carried out with *gram sarkar* which achieved very little success. Union parishads or subdistrict bodies were largely dominated by rural and urban elites. As a result, the peasantry in Bangladesh lacks a proper forum for the redressal of its grievances. In the absence of appropriate local power structure, the state carries out most of its development programme in collusion with the district-level bureaucracy and rural elites. This helps the rich peasant dominance in village affairs.

In the context of West Bengal, the unionization of peasants is an important factor in raising awareness. The process of unionization of the rural poor took a new turn when the CPI(M) peasant wing, the West Bengal Kisan Sabha, made an all out effort to spread its activity. A steep rise in the number of kisan sabha members could be noticed throughout the eighties in most parts of West Bengal. Some of the adverse effects of technological change, e.g. eviction of tenants, payment of low wages and land alienation have either been eliminated or minimized as a result of mobilization of the peasants. Kohli (1987) who examined the role of the state at length in bringing about changes in the agricultural sector in West Bengal emphasized the coherent nature of peasants leadership, the appropriate combination of centralized and decentralized arrangements, the exclusion of propertied classes

---

[6] See Lieten (1992b), *Westergaard* (1986).

from participation in governance and creation of stable and non-threatening atmosphere in which the propertied entrepreneurial class could invest were crucial factors in growth. In this process Kohli did take note of the shift from a revolutionary to reformist ideology. It was more of a social 'democratic' model of growth, observed Kohli.

Since Partition, the peasantry in Bangladesh has remained unorganized and isolated from the mainstream of national politics. Except the National Awami Party (NAP) of Moulana Bhasani and the Communist Party of Bangladesh (CPB), other political parties have hardly made attempts to organize the peasantry. The 'peasant question' remained in the background during the liberation movement in 1971. The Awami League and other major political parties were of the view that peasant organizations could lead to divisions among the rural masses and this was bound to affect the larger interests of national liberation.[7] However, even after two decades of political liberation, parties have remained indifferent towards the question of peasant organization. Such a situation helps in maintaining land-power nexus and in giving a free hand to the state and in following partisan policies. Thus, in spite of technological growth and improvement in agricultural production in some parts of Bangladesh, the issues relating to equity have not been resolved.

In one respect, however, the situation in Bangladesh looks promising. In many areas, the task of organizing the poor peasants has been taken over by the non-government organizations (NGOs). Unlike peasant organizations, the NGOs rely on persuasion rather than coercion in fulfilling their demands. Broadly, both types of organizations aim at raising awareness among the rural poor for their social and economic well-being. As long as the NGOs help the poor to perceive the 'relations of exploitation' or the power of the rural rich to withhold the right wage or the share of the produce or the power to use the law of the land to harass the poor, they go a long way in providing a new direction. As Freire (1972) noted, in the process the rural poor become conscious of their power too and they realize what they can do with their power. This is perhaps the most notable contribution of the NGOs to a vast, malleable and passive population of Bangladesh.

The experiments with agrarian reforms in West Bengal are unique in terms of state intervention, power relations and unionization of

[7] This is similar to the controversy which took place within the Congress Party at the time of Independence movement in India.

rural workers. It is unique also from the point of view of the role of small cultivators and sharecroppers in agricultural modernization. Diffusion of knowledge of technological innovation has been possible due to their active involvement in agricultural production. Some critics have expressed concern regarding sustainability of these reforms. Can the West Bengal experiment afford to ignore and resist the pressure of the market forces except at the risk of suppressing or slowing down the process of growth? It is not clear how agrarian reforms programmes in West Bengal are going to take shape in the near future and cope with the market forces. At this point, comments on this question are bound to be conjectural. The problem merits a close attention from all those who would be studying agrarian reforms in West Bengal in the coming decades.

Glossary

abad	cultivation
Agrahan	Bengali month, mid-November to mid-December
aman	Principal paddy crop in Bengal cultivated between July-August and December-January
aratdars	hoarder
Asar	Bengali month, mid-June to mid-July
Ashvin	Bengali month, mid-September to mid-October
Baisakh	Bengali month, mid-April to mid-May
bargadar	sharecropper
basat praja	non-occupancy tenant
beels	marsh, swamp
benami land	land illegally held by owners in violation of ceiling laws
Bhadra	Bengali month, mid-August to mid-September
bhagchasi	sharecropper
bigha	measuring unit of land, approximately one-third of an acre
boro	summer paddy crop grown between March and June
chakla	a revenue district during the Mughal period
chandina	non-occupancy tenant
darpatnidar	intermediary, under a *patnidar*
dhani krishak	rich peasant
garib chasi	poor peasant
gram sarkar	village council
grihasta chasi	family farmer
ijaradari	contractual arrangement on a fixed rent basis
Jyestha	Bengali month, mid-May to mid-June
jon majur	agricultural labourer
jotedar	intermediate tenure holder under zamindar (there are local variations)
korfa	occupancy tenant for a fixed term
kharif	crop season, beginning between May and July and

	end between September and October
kisan sabha	peasant association
khola majur	wage labourer work on a contractual basis
mouza	revenue village
Magh	Bengali month, mid-January to mid-February
maund	measuring unit of rice, 82 pounds
panchayat	village council
para	residential area in the village
pargana	a revenue district in Mughal and British period
paricharak	non-occupancy tenant
patnidar	intermediary
Paus	Bengali month, mid-December to mid-January
Phalgun	Bengali month, mid-February to mid-March
praja	non-occupancy tenant
rabi	crops sown between October and December and harvested between February and May
ryot	cultivator
rupee	Indian currency
sairat mahal	landed property other than land, such as water bodies, marketplaces, etc.
sarkar	a large revenue division in Mughal period
seer	a measure of weight, little less than a kilogram
sepatni	intermediary
shravan	Bengali month, mid-July to mid-August
taka	monetary unit in Bangladesh
taluks	administrative subdivision
thika majur	contract labourer
utbandi	non-occupancy tenant
zamindar	land-owner under permanent settlement
zamindari	rights of estate of zamindars

Appendices

APPENDIX I: DISTRICTWISE WBPKS MEMBERSHIP 1975-6 TO 1978-9

Districts	1975-6	1976-7	1977-8	1978-9
Midnapur	25,000	31,165	1,44,399	4,55,301
24 Parganas	41,896	86,752	2,25,293	5,29,109
Burdwan	35,337	40,500	2,11,221	4,21,542
Murshidabad	59,164	32,308	1,07,421	2,60,862
Hoogli	28,015	24,800	1,34,717	2,65,297
Bankura	1,289	16,373	6,55,192	1,39,392
Birbhum	16,267	17,016	49,053	1,18,146
Howrah	24,850	24,979	61,331	1,51,339
Nadia	15,033	14,809	55,180	1,19,920
Cooch Bihar	6,000	17,100	3,613	1,06,161
Purulia	5,886	9,600	33,366	52,358
West Dinajpur	8,306	11,331	38,633	80,132
Jalpaiguri	9,300	9,645	37,000	62,538
Malda	7,563	11,702	50,240	60,248
Darjeeling	2,666	3,446	18,333	23,364
Total	2,86,572	3,51,526	18,24,992	28,45,709

SOURCE: WBPKS Reports, 1975-9.

APPENDIX II: DISTRICTWISE MEMBERSHIP OF
WBPKS, 1979-80 TO 1982-3

Districts	1979-80	1980-1	1981-2	1982-3
Midnapur	5,97,871	7,82,616	9,26,025	8,92,934
24 Parganas	4,60,374	5,36,625	7,51,346	8,50,458
Burdwan	4,57,577	5,26,762	6,44,458	7,56,402
Murshidabad	3,62,200	4,50,000	5,27,426	5,57,116
Hoogli	2,71,701	3,35,412	3,84,500	4,62,446
Bankura	1,75,345	2,28,638	2,47,571	3,59,845
Birbhum	1,29,652	1,35,717	1,68,180	2,01,272
Howrah	1,55,862	1,70,357	1,60,000	1,90,949
Nadia	1,35,180	1,20,001	1,58,698	1,85,480
Cooch Bihar	10,447	1,34,012	1,56,186	1,74,041
Purulia	90,300	1,21,664	1,38,496	1,70,358
West Dinajpur	1,00,147	1,18,133	1,19,234	1,42,348
Jalpaiguri	73,054	96,606	1,24,175	1,30,032
Malda	32,253	52,000	70,004	73,512
Darjeeling	32,000	34,000	40,426	84,800
Total	30,83,963	38,42,543	46,16,725	52,31,993

SOURCE: WBPKS Reports, 1979-83.

APPENDIX III: ITEMWISE COST OF PRODUCTION OF HYV
AUS AND *BORO* IN A BIGHA OF LAND IN BIRA, 1988

1.	Labour: Ploughing	120	120
	Weeding	120	120
	Transplanting	90	130
	Harvesting	105	150
	Winnowing	60	80
2.	Seeds	40	50
3.	Fertilizers	135	165
4.	Pesticides and Spraying	56	90
5.	Irrigation	40	80
6.	Others	80	100
	(e.g. carrying cost)		
	Total	846	1085

APPENDIX IV: SELECTED AGRICULTURAL INDICATORS IN
BANGLADESH AND WEST BENGAL

Indicators	Bangladesh	West Bengal
Cropping Intensity (1984-5)	152.2	107.2
Area Under Irrigation (Percentage of Net Cropped Area in 1983-4)	20.0	23.0
Land-Man Ratio (1984-5)	0.27	0.32
Yield/Acre/Kg (1984-5)		
Rice	574	646
Jute	570	605

SOURCE: Siddiqui et al. (1987).

APPENDIX V: LAND USE PATTERN IN WEST BENGAL,
AND BANGLADESH, 1984-5

Indicators	Bangladesh		West Bengal	
	Total Area in '000 acres	%	Total Area in '000 acres	%
Net Cropped Area	21353	59.70	13556	63.6
Forests	5297	14.81	2858	13.4
Area Not Available for Cultivation	7193	20.11	3326	15.6
Current Fallows	1199	3.35	154	0.7
Cultivable Waste	721	2.01	1432	607
Total	35763	99.98	21326	100.00

SOURCE: Siddiqui et al. (1987).

Bibliography

Abdullah, A. (1976), 'Land Reform and Agrarian Change in Bangladesh', *Bangladesh Development Studies*, Vol. 4, No. 1, pp. 67-114.

Abdullah, A. *et al.* (1976), 'Agrarian Structure and the IRDP: Preliminary Considerations', *Bangladesh Development Studies*, Vol. IV, No. 2, April.

Alamgir, Mohiuddin (1979), *Bangladesh: A Case of Below Poverty Level Equilibrium Trap*, Bangladesh Institute of Development Studies, Dhaka.

Alavi, Hamza (1973), 'The State in Post-colonial Societies', in Gough, K. and H. Sharma (eds.), *Imperialism and Revolution in South Asia*, Monthly Review Press, New York.

Amin, Samir (1976), *Unequal Development: an Essay on the Social Formations of Capitalism*, The Harvester Press, Sussex.

Arens, Jenneke and Jos van Beurden (1977), *Jhagrapur: Poor Peasants and Women in a Village in Bangladesh*, Arens and van Beurden, Amsterdam.

Bagchi, Amiya Kumar (1982), *The Political Economy of Underdevelopment*, Cambridge University Press, Cambridge.

Bangladesh, Government of (1985), *Land Reforms Ordinance and Rules, 1984*, The Bengal Prinitng Works, Dhaka.

Bandyopadhyay, Arun (1981), 'An Analysis of Agricultural Credit with special Reference to Small Farmers in West Bengal', Ph.D. Thesis, University of Delhi.

Bandyopadhyay, D. (1979), 'West Bengal: Experience in Land Reform', *Mainstream,* Annual Number, pp. 29-31.

―――― (1993), 'Fourth General Elections of Panchayats in West Bengal', *Mainstream*, Vol. XXXI, No. 33, June 26, pp. 15-21.

Bandyopadhyay, Nripen (1975), 'Changing Forms of Agricultural Enterprise: A Note', *Economic and Political Weekly*, Vol. 10, No. 17, pp. 700-1.

―――― (1977), 'Causes of Sharp Increase in Agricultural Labourers, 1961-71: A Case Study of Social-Existence Forms of Labour in North Bengal', *Economic and Political Weekly*, Review of Agriculture, December, pp. A 111-A 126.

―――― (1981), 'Operation Barga and Land Reform Perspectives: A Discussive Review', *Economic and Political Weekly*, Vol. XVI, Nos. 25-6, pp. A 38-A 42.

―――― (1985), 'Evolution of Land Reforms Measures in West Bengal: A Report', *ILO Asian Employment Programme Working Paper*, Bangkok.

Bandyopadhyay, Nripen and Arabinda Biswas (1978), 'Problem of Labour Enterprise in West Bengal Agriculture', *Social Scientist*, Vol. 6, No. 67, pp. 25-49.

Bandyopadhyay, Sekhar (1990), *Caste, Politics and the Raj: Bengal, 1872-1937*, K.P. Bagchi & Co., Calcutta.

Bandyopadhyay, Sekhar and Abhijit Dasgupta (eds.) (1997), *Jati, Varna and Bangali Samaj* (in Bengali), Naya Udyog, Calcutta.

Bangladesh Water Development Board (1988), *Report on Farm Management Survey of Irrigation Projects under BWDB*, Director of Land and Water Use, Dhaka.

Baran, Paul (1957), *The Political Economy of Growth*, Monthly Review Press, New York.

Bardhan, Pranab (1970), 'Green Revolution and Agricultural Labourers', *Economic and Political Weekly*, Vol. V, Special No., pp. 1239-46.

Bardhan, Pranab K. and T.N. Srinivasan (1971), 'Crop Sharing Teanacy in Agriculture: A Theoretical and Empirical Analysis', *American Economic Review*, No. 61, Vol. I, pp. 48-64.

Basu, Timir (1976), 'CADP: No Plan for the Poor', *Economic and Political Weekly*, Vol. XI, No. 51, December, pp. 1951-5.

Bell, Clive (1977), 'Alternative Theories of Sharecropping: Some Tests Using Evidence from North East India', *Journal of Development Studies*, Vol. 13, No. 4, pp. 317-46.

Bengal, Government of (1927), *Bengal Commission on Agriculture in India, Report*, Volume V: Evidence Taken in the Bengal Presidency, Government Central Press, Bombay.

Bengal, Government of (1948), *Report of the Land Revenue Commision of Bengal*, Bengal Government Press, Alipore, Clacutta.

Bengal, Government of, Department of Agriculture and Industries (1940b), *Report of the Paddy and Rice Enquiry Committee*, Bengal Government Press, Alipore, Calcutta.

Beteille, Andre (1974), *Studies in Agrarian Social Strucuture*, Oxford University Press, Delhi.

Bhaduri, Amit, (1973), 'A Study of Agricultural Backwardness under Semi-feudalism', *Economic Journal*, Vol. 83, No. I, pp.120-37.

Bhaduri, Amit, H.Z. Rahman and Ann Lisbet Arn (1986), 'Persistence and Polarisation: A Study in the Dynamics of Agrarian Contradiction', *The Journal of Peasant Studies*, Vol. 13, No. 3, April, pp. 82-9.

Bharadwaj, Krishna (1974a), *Production Conditions in Indian Agriculture: a Study Based on Farm Management Surveys*, Cambridge University Press, Cambridge.

——— (1974b), 'Notes on Farm Size and Productivity', *Economic and Political Weekly*, Vol. 9, Review of Agriculture, March.

Bhaumik, Sankar Kumar (1993), *Tenancy Relations and Agrarian Development: a study of West Bengal*, Sage Publications, New Delhi.

Biswas, Santosh Kumar (1990), 'Refugee Rehabilitation in West Bengal with Special Reference to the District of Nadia', Ph.D. Thesis, University of Calcutta, Calcutta.

Blyn, G. (1966), *Agricultural Trends in India, 1891-1947*, University of Pennsylvania, Philadelphia.

Bose, Sugata (1986), *Agrarian Bengal: Economy, Social Structure and Politics, 1919-47*, Cambridge University Press, Cambridge.

Boyce, James (1986), 'Water Control and Agriculture Preference in Bangladesh: Some Further Results', *Bangladesh Development Studies*, Vol. 14, No. 14, pp. 1-35.

———— (1987), *Agrarian impasse in Bengal: Institutional Constraints to Technological Change*, Oxford University Press, Oxford.

———— (1989), 'Population Growth and Real Wages of Agricultural Labourers in Bangladesh', *The Journal of Development Studies*, Vol. 4, No. 25, pp. 467-89.

Byres, T.J. (1972), 'The Dialectics of India's Green Revolution', in K. Griffin (ed.), *The Political Economy of Agrarian Change*, Macmillian, London.

Chadha, G.K. and S.K. Bhaimik (1992), 'Changing Tenancy Relations in West Bengal: Popular Notions, Grassroot Realities' (in two parts), *Economic and Political Weekly*, Vol. XXVII, No. 19, May, pp. 1009-17 and Vol. XXVII, Nos. 20-1, May, pp. 1089-98.

Chakrabarti, P.K. (1990), *The Marginal Men*, Lumiere Books, Kalyani.

Chatterjee, Partha (1984), *Bengal 1920-1947: The Land Question*, Vol. I, K.P. Bagchi and Co., Calcutta.

Chattopadhyay, B. (1984), *Tenancy Reform, The Power Structure and the Role of Administration: An Evaluation of Operation Barga*, Cressida, Calcutta.

Chaudhuri, Benoy Bhusan (1969), 'Rural Credit Relations in Bengal 1859-1885', *Indian Economic and Social History Review*, Vol. 6, No. 3, pp. 203-57.

———— (1975), 'The Process of Depeasantisation in Bengal and Bihar, 1885-1947', *The Indian Historical Review*, Vol. 2, No. 1, pp. 105-65.

———— (1979), 'Agrarian Movements in Bengal and Bihar', in A.R. Desai (ed.), *Peasant Struggles in India*, Oxford University Press, Bombay.

———— (1980), 'Agrarian Relations: Eastern India', in D. Kumar and M. Desai (eds.), *Cambridge Economic History*, Vol. I, Cambridge University Press, Cambridge.

———— (1982), 'Agrarian Relations in Eastern India', in T. Raychanduri and I. Habib (eds.), *The Cambridge Economic History of India*, Vol. II, Combridge University Press, Cambridge.

———— (1984), 'Rural Power Structure and Agricultural Productivity in Eastern India, 1757-1947', in Meghnad Desai, S.H. Rudolph and Ashok Rudra (eds.), *Agrarian Power and Agricultural Productivity in South Asia*, Oxford University Press, Delhi.

Cheung, Steven, N.S. (1968), 'Private Property Rights and Share-cropping', *Journal of Political Economy*, Vol. 76, pp. 1107-22.

Chowdhury, Anwarullah (1978), '*A Bangladesh Village: a Study of Social Stratification*, Centre for Social Studies, Dhaka.

Communist Party of India (Marxist) (1967), *Task on the Kisan Front: Resolution of the Central Comittee*, CPI(M), New Delhi.

Danda, Ajit K. and Dipali (1971), *Development and Change in Besudha*, National Institute of Community Development, Hyderabad.

Dasgupta, Abhijit (1987), *Bengal Provincial Kisan Sabha: A Sociological Study of a Peasant Organization*, ICSSR Report, Agro-economic Research Centre, Delhi.

Dasgupta, Biplab (1982a), *Rural Development: The CADC Experience, CADC*, Government of West Bengal, Calcutta.

——— (1982b), *Some Aspects of Land Reform in West Bengal in Land Reform: Land Settlement Cooperatives*, UNFAO Publications, Rome.

——— (1984), 'Sharecropping in West Bengal: From Independence to Operation Barga', *Economic and Political Weekly*, Vol. 19, No. 26, 30 June, pp. A 85-A 96.

——— (1984), 'Agriculture Labour under Colonial, Semi-capitalist and Capitalist Conditions, *Economic and Political Weekly*, Vol. XIX, No. 39, 29 September, pp. A 129-A 148.

——— (1995), 'Institutional Reforms and Poverty Alleviation in West Bengal, *Economic and Political weekly*, Vol. XXX, Nos. 41 and 42, 14-21 October, pp. 2691-2702.

Davis Marvin, (1983), *Rank And Rivalry: The Politics of Inequality in Rural West Bengal*, Cambridge University Press, Cambridge.

Downs, Anthony (1957), *An Economic Theory of Democracy*, Harper and Row, New York.

Epstein, T. Scarlett (1962), *Economic Development and Social Change in South India*, Manchester University Press, Manchester.

Faidley, L. and M.C. Esmay, (1976), 'Introduction and Use of Improved Rice Varieties: Who Benefits', in R.D. Stevens (*et al.*) *Rural Development in Bangladesh and Pakistan*, The University Press of Hawaii, Honolulu.

Feldman, Shelley and Florence E. McCarthy, (1987), 'Persistence of the Small-holder, Withering Away of the Small Farmers: Comments on Bhaduri, Rahman and Arn', *Journal of Peasant Studies*, Vol. 14, No. 4, July, pp. 543-7.

Frank, Andre Gunder (1967), *Capitalism and Underdevelopment in Latin America*: Historical Studies of Chile and Brazil, New York, Monthly Review Press.

Frankel, Francine (1971), *India's Green Revolution: Economic Gains and Political Costs*, Princeton University Press, Princeton.

Freire, Paulo (1972), *Pedagogy of the Oppressed*, Penguin Books Ltd., Harmondsworth.

Garett, I.H.E (1910), *Bengal District Gazetteers: Nadia*, Government of Bengal Press, Calcutta.

Ghatak, Maitresh (1995), 'Reforms Incentives and Growth in West Bengal Agriculture', Paper Presented at the Workshop on *Agrarian Growth and Agrarian Structure in Contemporary West Bengal and Bangladesh*, 9-12 January, Calcutta.

Ghosh, Ajit (1981), *Agrarian Reform in Contemporary Developing Countries*, Croom Helm, London.

Ghosh, Ratan (1976), 'Effect of Agricultural Legislation on Land Distribution in West Bengal', *Indian Journal of Agricultural Economics*, Vol. 31, No. 3, pp. 40-6.

——— (1981), 'Agrarian Reform of the Left Front Government', *Economic and Political Weekly*, Vol. XVI, Nos. 25-6, June, pp. A 49-A 53.

Goodman, D. and M. Redclift, (1977), *From Peasant to Proletarian*, Basil Blackwell, Oxford.

Gough, Kathleen (1981), *Rural Society in South-east India*, Cambridge University Press, Cambridge.

Government of Bangladesh (1984), *Land Reforms, Ordinance and Rules*, The Bengal Printing Works, Dhaka.

Government of West Bengal (1953), *Final Report of Enquiry into the condition of Agricultural Labourers in West Bengal, 1946-47*, West Bengal Government Press, Alipore.

——— (1979), *Tebhaga Theke Operation Barga* (From Tebhaga to Operation Barga), Government Press, Calcutta.

——— (1985), *Seventh Workshop on Land Reforms*, Board of Revenue, Calcutta.

Greenough, Paul (1982), *Prosperity and Misery in Modern Bengal: The Famine of 1943-44*, Oxford University Press, New York.

Griffin, Keith (1974), *The Political Economy of Agrarian Change: an Essay on the Green Revolution*, The Macmillian Press Ltd., London.

Grindle, Merilee S., and John W. Thomas (1991), *Public Choices and Policy Change: The Political Economy of Reform in Developing Countries*, John Hopkins University Press, Baltimore.

Guha, Ranajit (1983), *Elementary Aspects of Peasant Insurgency in Colonial India*, Oxford University Press, Delhi.

Hamid, M.A., S.K. Saha, Rahman and A.J. Khar (1978), *Irrigation Technologies in Bangladesh: A Study in Some Selected Areas*, Department of Economics, Rajasthani University, Rajasthan.

Harriss, John (1993), 'What is Happening in Rural West Bengal? Agrarian Reform, Growth and Distribution, *Economic and Political Weekly*, Vol. XXVIII, No. 24, June, pp. 1237-47.

Hasan, F.R.M. (1985), 'Process in Landless Mobilization in Bangladesh: Theory and Practice (Mimeo), *Bangladesh Institute of Development Studies*, Dhaka.

Hoselitz, B.F. (1960), *Sociological Factors in Economic Development*, Free Press, Chicago.

Hossain, M. (1989), *Green Revolution in Bangladesh*, University Press Ltd., Dhaka.

———— (1993), *Sustainable Medium Term Development for Bangladesh*, Centre for Economic, Social and Environmental Research, Dhaka.

Hunter, H.H. (1875), *Statistical Account of Bengal*, Vol. 2, Trubner, London.

Ishikawa, S. (1967), *Economic Development in Asian Perspective*, Kinokuniya, Tokyo.

Islam, M.M. (1978), *Bengal Agriculture: 1920-1946*, Cambridge University Press, Cambridge.

Jahangir, B.K. (1979), *Differentiation, Polarization and Confrontation in Rural Bangladesh*, Centre for Social Studies, Dhaka.

Jannuzi, F. Thomasson and James T. Peach (1980), *The Agrarian Structure of Bangladesh: An Impediment to Development*, Westview Press, Boulder.

Jansen, E.J. (1979), 'Choice of Irrigation Technologies in Bangladesh: Implications of Dependency Relationship Between Rich and Poor Countries', *Journal of Social Studies*, No. 5, pp. 61-84.

Jose, A.V. (1984), 'Poverty and Income Distribution: The Case of West Bengal, in A.R. Khan *et al. Poverty in Rural Asia*, ILO, ARTEP, Bangkok.

Joshi, P.C. (1974), 'Land Reform and Agrarian Change in India and Pakistan Since 1947', *The Journal of Peasant Studies*, Vol. 1, Nos. 2 and 3 (in two parts).

———— (1975), *Land Reforms in India*, Allied Publishers Limited, Bombay.

Karat, Prakash (1988), *Foreign Funding and the Philosophy of Voluntary Organizations*, National Book Centre, New Delhi.

Khan, A.R. (1984), 'Real Wages of Agricultural Workers in Bangladesh', in A.R. Khan *et al. Poverty in Rural Asia*, ILO ARTEP, Bangkok.

———— (1990), 'Poverty in Bangladesh: A Consequences of and a Constraint on Growth', *The Bangladesh Development Studies*, Vol. XVIII, No. 3, September, pp. 19-34.

Khan, A.R. and M. Hossain (1989), *The Strategies of Development in Bangladesh*, MacMillan, Houndmills.

Khan, M. Mahmud (1987), 'A Note on Persistence and Polarisation', *Journal of Peasant Studies*, Vol. 14, No. 4, July, pp. 538-42.

Khasnobis, Ratan (1981), 'Operation Barga: Limits to Social Democratic Reformism', *Economic and Political Weekly*, Vol. XVI, Nos. 25-6, June, pp. A 43-A 48.

Khasnobis, Ratan and Jyotiprakash Chakraborty (1982), 'Tenancy, Credit and Agrarian Backwardness: Results of a Field Survey', *Economic and Political Weekly*, Review of Agriculture, Vol. 17, No. 1, March, pp. A 21-A 32.

Khasnobis, Ratan and Jyoti Prakash Chakraborty (1989), *Surplus Utilisation in Agriculture*, Concept Publishing Co., New York.

Kohli, Atul (1987), *The State and Poverty in India: The Polities of Reform*, Cambridge University Press, Cambridge.

Konar, Hare Krishna (1976), *Agrarian Problems of India*, National Book Agency, Calcutta.

———— (1977), *Nirbachita Rachana Sankalan* (Selected Works), Gour Saha, Calcutta.

Ladejinski, Wolf (1973), 'How Green is the Indian Green Revolution?' *Economic and Political Weekly*, Vol. 8, No. 52, December, pp. A 133-44.

———— (1977), '*Agrarian Reform as Unfinished Business*, ed. by Louis. J. Walinsky, Oxford University Press, New York.

Lieten, G.K. (1990), 'Depeasantization Discontinued: Land Reforms in West Bengal', *Economic and Political Weekly*, Vol. XXV, No. 40, October, pp. 2265-71.

———— (1992a), *Continuity and Change in Rural West Bengal*, Sage, New Delhi.

———— (1992b), 'Caste, Gender and Class in Panchayats: Case of Bardhaman, West Bengal', *Economic and Political Weekly*, Vol. XXVII, No. 29, July, pp. 1567-74.

Lipton, Michael (1977), *Why Poor People Stay Poor: a Study of Urban Bias in World Development*, Temple Smith, London.

———— (1991), 'The State-Market Dilemma, Civil Society and Structural Adjustment', *The Round Table*, Vol. 317, pp. 21-31.

Majumdar, D. (1978), *West Bengal District Gazetteer: Nadia*, Government of West Bengal, Calcutta.

Mallick, Ross (1992), 'Agrarian Reform in West Bengal: The End of an Illusion', *World Development*, Vol. 20, No. 5, pp. 735-50.

———— (1993), *Development Policy of a Communist Government: West Bengal Since 1977*, Cambridge University Press, Cambridge.

Marshall, A. (1920), *Principles of Economics*, Macmillan, London.

Mitra, A. (1953), *An Account of Land Management in West Bengal, 1870-1950*, Government of West Bengal, Calcutta.

Mitter, Swasti (1977), *Peasant Movements in West Bengal and their Impact on Agrarian Class Relations Since 1967*, Department of Land Economics, University of Cambridge, Cambridge.

Moore, Barrington, Jr. (1966), *The Social Origins of Dictatorship and Democracy: Lord and Peasant in the Making of the Modern World*, Boston, Beacon.

Moore, W.E. (1963), *Social Change*, Prentice Hall, Inc., New Jersey.

Mukherjee, K.M. (1957), *The Problems of Land Transfers*, Visva Bharati, Santiniketan.

Mukherjee, Ramkrishna (1957), *The Dynamics of a Rural Society*, Akademic Verlag, Berlin.

Nandy, S.C. (1986), *History of the Cossimbazar Raj in the Nineteenth Century*, Dev Al Pvt. Ltd., Calcutta.

Nicholas, Ralph W. (1962), 'Villages of the Bengal Delta', Ph.D. Dissertation, University of Chicago.

Paige, Jeffrey (1975), *Agrarian Revolution: Social Movements and Export Agriculture in the Underdeveloped World*, Free Press, New York.

Pakrasi, Kanti B. (1971), *The Uprooted: A Sociological Study of the Refugees of West Bengal, India*, Editions Indian, Calcutta.

Pandian, M.S.S. (1987), 'On the So-called Stability of Small Landowners in Bangladesh', *The Journal of Peasant Studies*, Vol. 14, July, pp. 534-7.

Patnaik, Utsa (1987), *Peasant Class Differentiation: a Study in Method with Special Reference to Haryana*, Oxford University Press, Delhi.

Poulantzas, N. (1973), *Political Power and Social Crisis*, New Left Books, London.

Pringle, J.M. and Kemm Am. (1928), *Final Report on the Survey and Settlement Operations in the District of Nadia, 1919-25*, BSBD, Calcutta.

Quaseem, M.A. (1978), 'Factors Affecting the Use of Fertilisers in Bangladesh', *Bangladesh Development Studies* Vol. 6, No. 3, Monsoon, pp. 300-38.

Ragin, Charles C. (1987), *The Comparative Method: Moving Beyond Qualitative and Quantitative Strategies*, University of California Press, Berkeley.

Rahman, Atiur (1986), *Irrigation in Two Comilla Villages*, Academy for Rural Development, Comilla.

——— (1986), *Peasants and Classes: A Study in Differentiation in Bangladesh*, Oxford University Press, Delhi.

Rao, A.P. (1967), 'Size of Holdings and Productivity', *Economic and Political Weekly*, Vol. 2, No. 11, November.

Rao, D.S.K. (1995), Farmers Management of Public Tubewells in West Bengal, *Economic and Political Weekly*, Vol. XXX, No. 39, 30 September.

Rasul, Abdullah (1969), *Krishak Sabhar Itihas* (A History of Krishak Sabha), National Book Agency, Calcutta.

——— (1974), *History of the All India Kisan Sabha*, National Book Agency, Calcutta.

Raychaudhuri, Ajitava and Airjit Chakraborty (1981), 'Sharecropping in West Bengal: Where it Stands Today', in M. Bose (ed.), *Land Reforms in Eastern India*, Papers and Proceedings of a Seminar held by the Planning Forum of the Jadavpur University from 4 February 1978, Jadavpur University, Calcutta.

Ray, Rajat and Ratna (1973), 'The Dynamics of Continuity in Rural Bengal under the British Imperium', *Indian Economic and Social History Review*, Vol. 10, No. 2, pp. 103-28.

Rostow, W.W. (1953), *The Process of Economic Growth*, Oxford University Press, London.

Rudolph Lloyd I. and Susanne Hoeber Rudolph (1984), 'Determinants and Varieties of Agrarian Mobilization', in Meghnad Desai, S.H. Rudolph and Ashok Rudra (eds.), *Agrarian Power and Agricultural Productivity in South Asia*, Oxford University Press, New Delhi.

Rudra, Ashok (1968), 'Farm Size and Yield Per Acre', *Economic and Political Weekly*, Special No., July.

————— (1970), 'In Search of Capitalist Farmers', *Economic and Political Weekly*, Vol. XI, No. 25-6, June, pp. 213-21.

————— (1981a), *Paschim Banger Bargadar* (Bargadars of West Bengal), Kathasilpa, Calcutta.

————— (1981b), 'One Step Forward, Two Steps Backward', *Economic and Political Weekly*, Vol. XVI, Nos. 25-6, June, pp. A 61-2.

————— (1982a), *Indian Agricultural Economics: Myths and Realities*, Allied Publishers, New Delhi.

————— (1982b), 'Land Reforms', *Frontier* Vol .4, No. 7, March.

Scott, James C. (1976), *The Moral Economy of the Peasant: Rebellion and Subsistence in South East Asia*, Yale University Press, New Haven.

Sen, A.K. (1964), 'Size of Holdings and Productivity', *The Economic Weekly*, Vol. XVI, Nos. 5, 6 and 7, 4 February.

Sen, S.B. (1983), *Composition of West Bengal Panchayats: a Survey Report*, Govt. of West Bengal, Calcuta.

Sen, Sunil (1972), *Agrarian Struggle in Bengal: 1946-47*, People's Publishing House, New Delhi.

Sengupta, Nirmal (1991), *Managing Common Property: Irrigation in India and the Phileipines*, Sage, New Delhi.

Shah, Tushaar (1993), *Ground Water Markets and Irrigation Development: Political Economy and Practical Policy*, Oxford University Press, Bombay.

Siddiqui, A. (1976), *Bangladesh District Gazetteers: Kushtia*, Bangladesh Government Press, Dhaka.

Siddiqui, K. (1979), 'Review of Bengal Agriculture, 1920-46: A Quantitative Study', *Journal of Social Studies*, No. 43, pp. 107-14.

Siddiqui, K., Imam Hossain, Zahirul Islam, Najmul Islam Chowdhury and Abdul Moomen (1988), *Land Reforms and Land Management in Bangladesh and West Bengal*, University Press Limited, Dhaka.

Smith, D.V. (1975), 'New Seeds and Income Distribution in Bangladesh', *The Journal of Development Studies*, Vol. 11, No. 2, pp. 162-86.

Smelser, N.J. (1959), *Social Change in the Industrial Revolution*, Routledge and Kegan Paul, London.

Sobhan, Rehman (1993), 'Structural Maladjustments: Bangladesh's Experience with Market Reforms', *Economic and Political Weekly*, Vol. XXVIII, No. 19, May, pp. 925-31.

Standing, G. (1982), *Circulation and Proletarianization*, WEF Research Working Paper, ILO, Geneva.

Streeten, Paul (1993), 'Markets and States: Against Minimalism', *World Development*, Vol. 21, No. 8, pp. 1281-98.

Thomas, J.W. (1965), 'The Choice of Technologies for Irrigation Tubewells in East Pakistan: An Analysis of a Development Policy Decision', in

C. Timmer *et al. The Choice of Technology in Developing Countries: Some Cautionary Tasks*, Harvard Studies in International Affairs, Cambridge.

Tilly, Charles (1981), *As Sociology Meets History*, Academic Press, New York.

van Schendel, Willem (1982), *Peasant Mobility: The Odds of Life in Rural Bangladesh*, Manohar, Delhi.

————— (1991), *Three Deltas: Accumulation and Poverty in Rural Burma, Bengal and South India*, Sage, New Delhi.

————— (1993), 'Easy Come, Easy Go: Smugglers on the Ganges', *Journal of Contemporary Asia*, 23:2, pp. 189-213.

van Schendel, Willem and Aminul Haque Faraizi (1984), *Rural Labourers in Bengal 1880 to 1980*, Erassmus University, Comparative Asian Studies Programme, Rotterdam.

Vylder, Stefan de (1982)., *Agriculture in Chains — Bangladesh: a Case Study in Contradictions and Constraints*, Zed Press, London.

Wallerstein, Immanuel (1974), *The Modern World System: Capitalist Agriculture and the Origins of the European World Economy in the Sixteenth Century*, Academy Press, New York.

————— (1979), *The Capitalist World Economy*, Cambridge University Press, Cambridge.

Webster, Neil (1990), 'Agrarian Relations in Burdwan District, West Bengal: From the Economics of Green Revolution to the Politics of Panchayati Raj', *Journal of Contemporary Asia*, Vol. XX, No. 2, pp. 177-211.

Westergaard, Kirsten (1986), *People's Participation, Local Government and Rural Development: The Case of West Bengal, India*, Centre for Development Research, Copenhagen.

Wolf, Eric R. (1969), *Peasant Wars of the Twentieth Century*, Harper and Row, New York.

————— (1982), *Europe and the People Without History*, University of California Press, Berkeley.

Wood, G.D. (1976), 'Class Differentiation and Power in Bandakgram: the Minifundist Case, in M.A. Huq (ed.), *Exploitation and the Rural Poor, Bangladesh Academy for Rural Development*, Comilla.

Index

Abdullah, A. 122
Alavi, Hamza 28
Arens, Jenneke 136
Arn, Ann Lisbet 121
Awami League Government, and land reform legislations 120
Awami League Party 159

Bandyopadhyay, D. 23, 84, 115
Bandyopadhyay, Nripen 104, 106, 109
Bandyopadhyay, Sekhar 82
Bangladesh, absence of peasant associations and *panchayats* in 150, 158, 159; agricultural growth in 127, 156; expansion of irrigation in 123-5, 156; 'green revolution' belts of 125; *gram sarkars* (GSs) in 151; infant mortality rate in 118; land reforms in 119, 120; landlessness in 122; literacy in 118; malnutrition among children in 118; new agricultural technologies and employment opportunities in 147; NGOs in 151-2, 159-60; *panchayats* in 150, 158, 159; and the 1976 Pilot Agricultural Census 121; poverty situation in 118; use of High Yielding Varieties (HYV) seeds and fertilisers in 124-6; worsening conditions for agricultural labourers in 148-50, 156
Bangladesh Academy of Rural Development (BARD) 20, 127, 128
Bangladesh Agricultural Development Council (BADC) 20
Bangladesh Agricultural Research Council (BARC) 20

Bangladesh Bhumihin Samiti 151
Bangladesh Krishi Bank 124
Bangladesh Land Reforms Ordinance, 1984 120
Bangladesh Leaf Tobacco Company 144
Bangladesh Rice Research Institute (BRRI) 124
Bangladesh Rural Advancement Committee (BRAC) 29, 151
Bangladesh Water Development Board (BWDB) 123, 129
Baran, Paul 27
Bardhan, Pranab K. 72, 109, 111
Bell, Clive 72, 101
Bengal, expansion of irrigation facilities in 17, 18; extensive use of HYV seeds, fertilisers and pesticides in 17-18, 20; 'green revolution' belts of 17; growth of agriculture in 17, 22, 154; land reforms in 24, 26; landlessness in 23; partition of 31, 154; percentage of sharecroppers in 23, 37; problem of equity in 22, 23
Bengal land Revenue Commission Report 37
Bengal Provincial Krishak Sabha (BPKS) of the CPI (M) 81
Bengal Tenancy Act of 1885 43
Betteile, Andre 23
Bhaduri, Amit 106, 121
Bharadwaj, Krishna 98, 156
Bhaumik, Sankar Kumar 105, 106, 107
Block Development Offices (BDOs) 20
Blyn, G. 36